D0901416

The Core Elements of Priestly Formation Programs: A Collection of Readings

VOLUME 4

This series is a collection of previously published articles that offer the "best practices" and wisdom and insight of a wide variety of seminary professionals and church leaders. Most of them come from the *Seminary Journal*.

The *Seminary Journal* is a journal of opinion, research, and praxis in the field of seminary education and formation for priesthood within the Roman Catholic tradition. Articles are selected, edited, and published by the executive director of the Seminary Department of the National Catholic Educational Association.

Bro. Bernard F. Stratman, SM, *Executive Editor*
Michael Coombe, *Editor*
Beatrice Ruiz, *Graphic Designer*

Distribution Policy

Seminary Journal is published 3 times per year: spring, fall and winter. NCEA Seminary Department members are entitled to 4 copies of the *Seminary Journal*. They are mailed to the president/rector, the academic dean, the director of formation, and the librarian. Additional copies may be purchased.

Disclaimer

Views expressed in the articles are those of the respective authors and not necessarily of NCEA or the Seminary Department.

Index to Seminary Journal

The journal is indexed in The Catholic Periodical and Literature Index.

For an online index of articles featured in *Seminary Journal* since 1995 go to www.ncea.org/departments/seminary.

Published by the National Catholic Educational Association
1077 30th Street, NW, Suite 100
Washington, DC 20007-3852

ISBN   1-55833-360-6
Part No.   SEM-17-1354

The Core Elements of Priestly Formation Programs: A Collection of Readings

VOLUME 4

Contents

Preface

The Core Elements of Priestly Formation Programs: A Collection of Readings

In recognition of the 10th anniversary of *Seminary Journal*, the Seminary Department has introduced a new publication series, *The Core Elements of Priestly Formation Programs: A Collection of Readings*. This collection of articles from *Seminary Journal* celebrates the "best practices" and wisdom and insight of a wide variety of seminary professionals and church leaders. A number of articles are drawn from sources other than the journal. Some of the older articles have been updated. Others are new to the journal but will be featured in forthcoming issues.

The *Core Elements* series is an ongoing publishing effort. New collections of readings will be added annually. The framework for the first three booklets is the four pillars identified in the bishops' Program of Priestly Formation: *Intellectual, Spiritual, Human,* and *Pastoral*. The fourth addresses the topic of addictions, an issue of increasing significance to formators today.

The booklets were produced as an in-service resource for faculty and staff, for personal study, and as a source book of readings for those in formation.

Our goal is to add one or more booklets to this series annually. The list of topics being considered for 2006 and 2007 includes: philosophy in the seminary curriculum, media and technology in theological education, screening and testing issues, spiritual formation, programs of priestly formation for older candidates and international seminarians, and more.

This creative enterprise would not be possible without the financial support of our membership and ministry colleagues. These contributions and the advance purchases received make it possible to publish these booklets. In particular, we would like to thank Father Melvin Blanchette, SS, director of the Institute for the Formation of Seminary Formation Staff and Advisors and a member of the formation team at Theological College, for his personal commitment to the development of this project. We would also like to recognize and express our appreciation to Guest House for its continued support and generosity toward the work of the department. Likewise, we wish to acknowledge the growing list of member seminaries that signed on as project sponsors: St. Lawrence Seminary High School, Moreau Seminary, The Pontifical North American Seminary, Conception College Seminary, St. Mary Seminary and Graduate School of Theology, St. Joseph's Seminary (Dunwoodie), St. Charles Seminary (El Paso, Tex.), St. Joseph's Seminary (Josephites/Sacred Heart), and St. Paul's College (Paulists).

We welcome your feedback and recommendations for the future development of this initiative.

Bernard F. Stratman, SM
Executive Director
Seminary Department

The Good News Can Flourish Only in Good Soil

Daniel A. Kidd

This article is reprinted from Seminary Journal, *Volume 9, Winter 2003.*

Almost fifty years have passed since the American Medical Association officially acknowledged the disease of alcoholism, a definition that accelerated the acceptance of alcoholics and their treatment as opposed to their punishment. That definition came in 1954, and in 1956 Guest House opened in Lake Orion, Michigan, with an approach to alcoholism so innovative that only two bishops were open to receiving Guest House. One was Edward Cardinal Mooney of Detroit. By 1958, Guest House already had proven its effectiveness, so much so that it had a waiting list for priests to be admitted. By 1964, the waiting list was two years long. Hence, the modern approach to treatment of priests was accepted, and the rest is history. Treatment seems encouraging and more accepted for the addicted ones, but it begs the question of whether addictions can be prevented, not just treated.

Whether this disease or any other addiction is preventable is debated in the circles of alcoholism. The genetic basis of alcoholism seems well accepted, so how does one prevent a genetic illness? The answer is in the interplay of addiction with culture.

The relevance of this to this issue of the *Seminary Journal* is that the formation of holy, healthy, and effective priests is a high priority both for the leadership of the church and also for its people in the pews. The desire of Catholics for a healthy presbyterate is particularly strong given the recent history of sexual misconduct, some of which seems associated with the use or abuse of alcohol or other drugs. In addition, our priests of the future need to possess knowledge and skills to deal with addiction in pastoral situations which priests may confront on a daily basis.

> **"We would have a healthier church if there were less alcoholism, compulsive sexual behavior, compulsive gambling, overeating, and drug abuse (legal and illegal)."**

There are cultural aspects that affect the development of alcoholism and other drug addictions, just as environmental factors contribute to the manifestation of other genetically based diseases. There are few cause-and-effect aspects of most biological diseases, much less of those that are behavioral or psychological. There are mostly just correlations, but correlations can be helpful.

For example, ethnic groups that tolerate excessive alcohol consumption have more alcoholism than groups in which over drinking is taboo. So if a person is born with a gene for alcoholism and grows up in a culture that accepts excessive drinking, he or she is more likely to become an alcoholic. The correlation is positive.

Ethnic groups in which the pressure to drink is strong have more problems with alcoholism. Groups where members begin drinking at an earlier age have more problems with drinking than those who delay. The more available alcohol or drugs is in any group, the more problems will occur. Harvard researcher Dr. George Vaillant amply describes these social and cultural factors in *The Natural History of Alcoholism.* The same principles probably apply to other addictions as well, although research is limited.

We are living in a culture of excesses in almost everything. Tolerance of excesses in things like spending, eating, and sex is actually rewarded with recognition and peer approval. The pressure to engage in potentially addictive behaviors is strong. Try turning down a drink offer and see what transpires. The Internet has made possible secretive gambling and sexual behaviors in virtually an unlimited way. There seem to be few or no community standards regarding obscenity, as the United States Supreme Court once thought existed in our culture; hence, there are no controls.

We have all-you-can-eat buffets, happy hours with free alcohol, hundreds of television channels, casinos and riverboats where once there was only Las Vegas. The culture supports excess, and excess supports addiction.

What does this have to do with the church is 2004? Well, we would have a healthier church if there were less alcoholism, compulsive sexual behavior, compulsive gambling, overeating, and drug abuse (legal and illegal). And we desperately want to have a future with less of the pain that victims, both personal and corporate, have been experiencing. A healthier presbyterate means a church that can focus on the New Evangelization called for by the Holy Father. This evangelization includes dealing with the issues of addiction, because the Good News can flourish only in good soil.

"The seminary must see a role for itself much greater than merely the training of professional priests."

The seminary plays a vital role in this aspect of human formation. More attention paid to this issue will reap massive rewards for a healthier church. The culture of the seminary itself needs to contribute to moderation, not excess. The seminary needs to recognize factors that contribute to addiction, including the family background, genetic component, and social and cultural attitudes that correlate with addiction problems.

Above all, the seminary must see a role for itself much greater than merely the training of professional priests. The salvation of souls of seminarians, priests, religious, and the laity is a serious matter. The New Evangelization includes having priests who can relate effectively with those to whom they minister when approached with problems of addiction in the sacrament of reconciliation or in pastoral counseling situations. These skills are teachable in the seminary.

Austin Ripley, the founder of Guest House, spent considerable time in seminaries in the early years of his treatment center. He went to seminaries for three reasons: to prevent alcohol problems, to make future intervention on an alcoholic priest more palatable if needed, and to develop awareness by future priests of the alcoholism problems they would encounter in their flocks. All of these needs are no less important today than in 1956.

Daniel A. Kidd is president of Guest House, an addiction treatment center for Catholic clergy and religious in Lake Orion, Michigan.

Religion, Science and Substance Abuse: Why Priests and Psychiatrists Should Get Their Act Together

Joseph A. Califano, Jr.

This article is reprinted from Seminary Journal, *Volume 9, Winter 2003.*

If ever the sum were greater than the parts, it is in combining the power of God, religion, and spirituality with the power of science and professional medicine to prevent and treat substance abuse and addiction. That's the good news from "So Help Me God: Substance Abuse, Religion and Spirituality," the two-year study released in November 2001 by the National Center on Addiction and Substance Abuse (CASA) at Columbia University. The bad news is how few clergy get any substance abuse training and how many psychiatrists and other healthcare providers refuse to take advantage of the power of spirituality and religion to prevent and treat this disease.

America has a unique tradition of religious commitment: Almost all our people profess a belief in God and 92% affiliate with a particular religion. An astonishing array of churches and cathedrals, synagogues, Islamic centers and mosques, and Hindu and Buddhist temples enrich our states.

America is the most medically advanced nation in the world. Cities across the country house the most sophisticated hospital and health care complexes and equipment. Our physician

> **"Individuals in successful recovery commonly display greater levels of faith and spirituality than those who relapse."**

training has given us the finest medical professionals. Yet clergy and physicians, religion and science, are too often ships passing in the night. When we separate the worlds of medicine and spirituality, we deny a host of individuals help that may aid their recovery and ease their pain—especially with respect to substance abuse and addiction. One need only listen to the eloquent voices of persons in recovery as they speak about the role of God and spirituality in their own healing processes.

The CASA report, including unprecedented surveys of clergy and heads of schools of theology, documents the enormous power of God, religion, and spirituality in preventing and treating substance abuse. Here are some examples.

- Adults who do not consider religious beliefs important are more than one and one-half times likelier to smoke, more than three times likelier to binge drink, almost four times likelier to use an illicit drug other than marijuana, and more than six times likelier to smoke pot than adults who believe that religion is important.

- Adults who never attend religious services are three times likelier to smoke, more than five times likelier to use an illicit drug other than marijuana, almost seven times likelier to binge drink, and almost eight times likelier to smoke pot than those who attend religious services at least weekly.

- Teens who do not consider religious beliefs important are almost three times likelier to drink, binge drink, and smoke; almost four times likelier to use marijuana; and seven times likelier to use illicit drugs than teens who believe that religion is important.

- Teens who never attend religious services are twice as likely to drink, more than twice as likely to smoke, more than three times likelier to use marijuana and binge drink, and almost four times likelier to use illicit drugs than teens who attend religious services at least weekly.

- College students with no religious affiliation are more likely to binge drink than those who identify themselves as Catholics or Protestants.

- The one-third of prison inmates who participate in religious activities exhibit lower rates of recidivism—and recidivism is due almost entirely to drug and alcohol abuse.

Religion and spirituality can be important, sometimes determinative companions to the treatment and recovery process. Many recovering alcoholics and addicts attribute their motivation to seek treatment and their ability to maintain sobriety to their religious beliefs and the support of a community of believers. Individuals who attend spiritually based 12-step programs such as Alcoholics Anonymous (AA) and Narcotics Anonymous (NA) and receive treatment are more likely to maintain sobriety. Individuals in successful recovery commonly display greater levels of faith and spirituality than those who relapse.

In view of the significance of religion to prevention and treatment, the most troubling

discoveries of the CASA study are two profound disconnects: one, between the extent to which clergy see substance abuse as a problem among congregations and families they serve and their lack of knowledge and training in the area; the other, between the importance of God, religion and spirituality to effective treatment and the medical profession's failure to tap into this resource in ministering to substance abusers and addicts.

> **"Yet, only 12.5% of clergy received any substance abuse training during their theological studies. Only 36% said they preach a sermon addressing the issue more than once a year."**

The Clergy Disconnect

Of the priests, ministers, and rabbis* surveyed, 94% of frontline clergy and 98% of theology school presidents consider substance abuse and addiction an important problem in their congregations. Yet, only 12.5% of clergy received any substance abuse training during their theological studies. Only 36% said they preach a sermon addressing the issue more than once a year. (I have attended Mass more than 4,000 times during my life and I can remember only one occasion where a priest discussed the subject in a sermon: Father Thomas Bennett at Our Lady of Perpetual Help in Washington Depot, Connecticut.) These survey responses are deplorable since alcohol and drug abuse are so implicated in child and spousal abuse, violent crime, rape, teen pregnancy, sexually transmitted diseases, family breakup and divorce, school dropout and failure, debilitating accidents and job loss—all problems that clergy confront every day in their congregations.

The Provider-Patient Disconnect

Equally disturbing is the lack of recognition among health care providers—especially psychiatrists, psychologists, and other mental health professionals—of the importance of God, religion, and spirituality to treating patients struggling with substance abuse and addiction. Only 40% to 45% of mental health practitioners believe in God. Only 37% of psychiatrists responded affirmatively to the question, "If it were scientifically demonstrated that the use of a spiritual intervention (e.g., prayer) improved patient progress, would you perform that intervention?" Only 57% of psychiatrists would recommend that a patient consult a member of the clergy. Sixty-five percent of psychiatrists report that religion and spiritual issues were rarely or never included in their training.

For a sense of the chasm between these mental health care providers and patients consider these facts: 95% of Americans believe in God; 79% believe that spiritual faith can help people recover from disease, including addiction; and 70% think that physicians should talk to patients about spiritual faith.

The Combination Opportunity

Clergy are a barely tapped resource in preventing and treating substance abuse and addiction. Priests, ministers, rabbis, imams, and other religious leaders should become more engaged in addressing this problem by preaching about substance abuse issues and incorporating prevention and recovery messages in their ministry. Many individuals—especially Catholics and some Protestants—turn to their parish priest or minister for help in dealing with substance abuse problems. Schools of theology and seminaries—Protestant, Catholic, Rabbinical, and others—should educate their students to recognize the signs of substance abuse and how to deal with them. Clergy should become familiar with treatment services available in their communities.

Santa Fe Archbishop Michael J. Sheehan is showing the way. He has held an Archbishop's Forum on Drug Abuse in four cities in New Mexico and issued an All Saints Day pastoral letter in November 2001 setting out action plans for individuals, young persons, families, parishes, and the archdiocese based on, as he put it, "The good news...that people who are enslaved and blinded by drugs [including alcohol] can be freed through the amazing saving grace of Jesus Christ." This remarkable spiritual leader urges parishes to "keep a list of treatment centers and their phone numbers handy for referral purposes when the need arises." Archbishop Sheehan sees substance abuse as "the number one health problem in New Mexico" and is mounting a program that sets an example for every archdiocese of how to combine the power of the spiritual and the scientific.

Healing the Disconnect

Psychiatrists and other mental health providers are of course free to hold their own agnostic and atheistic beliefs, but they should be better trained and informed of the potential of God, spirituality, and religion to help prevent and treat substance abuse and addiction. They should learn of the spiritual and religious resources available in their local communities and how to take advantage of them. Health care providers should not shy away from discussing their patients' spiritual needs and desires; they should be prepared to refer patients to appropriate clergy or spirituality-based programs to assist their recovery. Perhaps the head of some local chapter of a mental health organization, like the American Psychiatric Association, will take a cue from Archbishop Sheehan's outreach effort in New Mexico.

A better understanding by the clergy of the disease of alcohol and drug abuse and addiction—together with a better appreciation by the medical profession, especially psychiatrists and psychologists, of the power of God, religion, and spirituality to help patients with this disease—offers a gold mine for prevention and treatment that can help millions of Americans and their families.

To take advantage of the potentially positive benefits of religion and spirituality to prevent substance abuse, intervene in its progress, and help individuals recover from its effects, I make the following recommendations:

- Protestant, Catholic, rabbinical, and other seminaries and schools of theology should train clergy to recognize the signs and symptoms of substance abuse and know how to respond, including referral to treatment and strategies for relapse prevention. These schools should provide basic educational and clinical knowledge of the short- and long-term effects of tobacco, alcohol, and other drugs and educate their students about ways to incorporate prevention messages both formally and informally into their work. They should educate their students about the co-occurrence with substance abuse of mental health and other problems (such as domestic violence and child abuse). These schools should include courses related to substance abuse in degree requirements and provide in-service training for current clergy.

- Clergy members who have completed their formal education should take advantage of additional substance abuse training in order to be knowledgeable about the topic. Resources include: local public substance abuse treatment agencies, private licensed substance abuse professionals, substance abuse professional organizations such as the National Association of State Alcohol and Drug Agency Directors (NASADAD), federal resources such as the National Institute on Drug Abuse and the National Institute on Alcohol Abuse and Alcoholism, the U.S. Department of Health and Human Services Substance Abuse and Mental Health Services Administration and its Centers for Substance Abuse Prevention and Substance Abuse Treatment

- Members of the clergy should preach about substance abuse issues and informally include messages about the problem throughout their organization's programs, services, and counseling. Even religious services with assigned readings and themes can incorporate messages about substance abuse in sermon examples and pray for those addicted. Recognizing that substance abuse affects individuals and families in all congregations, clergy can inform their members with prevention messages, help connect members of their community to needed intervention and treatment resources, and, as many presently do, open their facilities to AA and NA meetings.

- Members of the clergy should reach out to treatment programs to offer spiritual support to individuals who desire such assistance. Clergy can help educate treatment providers about the promising effects of spirituality and religion in recovery. Clergy should learn about treatment programs in their communities. By building this relationship, clergy will know who to refer members to for treatment and know how to support referrals from treatment providers of clients seeking to deepen their spiritual life.

More research is needed to evaluate and increase the efficacy of faith-based prevention initiatives and treatment programs, develop better ways of measuring adolescent spirituality and religiousness, and document pathways through which religion and spirituality work to prevent substance abuse and aid in recovery.

> **"Clergy can help recovering individuals navigate these issues and benefit from a connection to a loving God and religious community."**

Participants in recovery may have great need for spiritual guidance. Individuals struggling to recover may feel abandoned by God or alienated from God or the religious community. Clergy can help recovering individuals navigate these issues and benefit from a connection to a loving God and religious community. For many individuals working to shake the shackles of addiction and hang on to sobriety, sound advice might well be this: Work at it as though everything depends on you and pray as though everything depends on God. That's not bad advice for priests and physicians as well.

Joseph A. Califano, Jr. is president of the National Center on Addiction and Substance Abuse at Columbia University. He was U.S. Secretary of Health, Education, and Welfare from 1977 to 1979.

Role of the Clergy: The Effects of Alcohol and Drugs on the Person and the Family

Reverend C. Roy Woodruff, Ph.D.

This article is reprinted from Seminary Journal, *Volume 9, Winter 2003. To obtain the full NACoA report, visit www.nacoa.org.*

There is no question that the need is there—in all parishes—for priests who know how to help those in their charge who struggle with personal addiction or the addiction of a loved one. After all, there are so many who need this kind of help. Alcoholism and other forms of chemical dependency are major, pervasive public health problems that are responsible for the death and ill health of millions of Americans each year, and profound confusion and suffering by their families and children.[1]

No segment of society is immune. While the patterns of addiction and its specific practical consequences may be different in wealthy suburbs, the inner city, and rural areas, the problem nevertheless cuts across all economic, social, and religious divides. And the harm extends beyond the alcoholic or drug-using individual to the entire social network dependent on him or her. Addiction is definitely a family disease, not only because there is a demonstrated genetic component, causing it to run in families, but also because of the way all family relationships are distorted in response to the addicted individual's behavior.[2]

Children who grow up in alcoholic or drug-dependent homes are especially vulnerable.[3] An unstable family life places their entire future well being in jeopardy. More than other children, they are prone to physical illness and injury, emotional disturbances, educational deficits, and behavior problems. In addition, these children are at high risk for alcoholism or drug abuse in later life. Every parish must be concerned about children like these in its care.

The question is, "How can today's priest be trained to fill the needs of individuals, families, and children affected by alcohol or drug dependence?" A new project is underway, with input from clergy of diverse faiths, that hopefully will provide some answers.

> **"People in all walks of life are getting better by means of attitudes and practices they define as spiritual."**

Addiction and Spirituality

There is a growing recognition, both inside and outside the framework of traditional religion, that there is a spiritual dimension to addiction. Christopher D. Ringwald, a journalist who covers drug treatment issues, has recently documented the fact that people in all walks of life are getting better by means of attitudes and practices they define as spiritual. His book, *The Soul of Recovery*, draws on interviews with some 300 alcoholics, addicts, experts, counselors, and family members in order to demonstrate that spirituality or God is "where the real action [is] in the treatment and recovery of people addicted to drugs."[4]

In an earlier study, also based on in-depth interviews, I found that alcoholics who had had a spiritual conversion experience during their addictive behavior gained an enormous resource for recovery which was transformational in their ability to gain and maintain sobriety.[5] I also found that those who became active in a parish relationship, in addition to an AA group, clearly had greater resources for spiritual growth, enhanced personal relationships, and a healthier attitude toward themselves and God.

> ## "A study...has found that religion and spirituality can lower the risk of addiction."

Similarly, a study conducted by the National Center on Addiction and Substance Abuse (CASA) at Columbia University has found that religion and spirituality can lower the risk of addiction among adolescents and adults, and that it can be an important factor in people's recovery.[6]

Gerald G. May, the author of *Addiction and Grace*, suggests another connection between addiction and spirituality.[7] He sees addictive behavior, or any unhealthy attachment, as a sign of spiritual malaise. Recovery, in this paradigm, means the loosening of all attachments, replacing them by the love of God.

Whether or not one accepts this understanding of recovery, it is obvious that the presence of a chemical addiction is a barrier to spirituality. One cannot choose freely and behave responsibly while under the influence of alcohol or psychoactive drugs; moreover, the need for these drugs tends to displace all other values in an individual's life.

Barriers to the Training of Priests

If addiction is a spiritual problem, and if spirituality is potentially an important contributor to recovery, one would think the subject would fall squarely within a priest's scope of responsibilities. Unfortunately, however, clergy in many if not most major U.S. religious faith groups and denominations feel poorly equipped to deal with the problem as it presents itself in their congregations. CASA surveyed clergy around the country and found that while virtually all the priests, ministers, and rabbis surveyed (94.4 percent) considered addiction to be an important issue that they confront, only a small minority (12.5 percent) had done any coursework on the subject during their theological studies.[8]

There are complex reasons for this state of affairs. A surface explanation is competition for space in the curriculum. Seminaries traditionally have focused on theology, philosophy, and the art of preaching; pastoral counseling is a recent addition and must include the entire spectrum of personal and family issues. Addiction is a complex, difficult subject, and it may not seem feasible to do it justice within severe time constraints.

Another possible explanation is that because the prevailing model of addiction emphasizes its biochemistry, counseling and treatment have become the province of health professionals. Those designing seminary curricula may have decided to leave the issue to these experts. But the CASA report judges that this attitude has created a "disconnect" between faith leaders' awareness of the severity of the problem and its spiritual ramifications, and the development within faith communities of the knowledge and skills needed to address the problem. CASA finds a comparable disconnect in the thinking of health professionals, who acknowledge that religion and spirituality are important aids to recovery, but who generally have not taken advantage of these important assets in dealing with the disease.

There may be other reasons why seminaries do not work more actively to address problems of alcohol and drug dependence. Addiction is a chronic disease, requiring long-term commitment to an individual's treatment, the support of his or her recovery, and the support of other individuals who are affected. If there is no model of an effective course of action that can be pursued within the limits of a priest's time and energy, it is unlikely that much will be done.

> **"If there is no model of an effective course of action that can be pursued within the limits of a priest's time and energy, it is unlikely that much will be done."**

Yet, as the CASA report points out, the failure of pastoral leaders to become involved is unfortunate. Churches, synagogues, mosques, and temples are basic institutions where people find support in their difficulties in life. If a family is in trouble and its faith community looks the other way, its members may draw the conclusion that they are being rejected, or that their religion has nothing useful to offer them.

The CASA report recommended a series of measures, beginning with the expansion of seminary training on the subject of addiction, to overcome the multiple disconnects between awareness and action.

Developing a Set of Core Competencies

The Johnson Institute (JI) and the National Association for Children of Alcoholics (NACoA), recognizing the need to develop an adequate knowledge and skill base for clergy, convened a panel of experts to study the faith community's role in this area and to recommend ways clergy training on the subject could be enhanced. JI has forty years' experience in the design and implementation of programs of early intervention and recovery from alcoholism, and has always viewed alcoholism as an illness that affects the entire family. For nearly 25 years, NACoA has been the leading advocate on behalf of children of alcohol or drug-dependent parents.

This interdenominational panel, which met in Baltimore, Maryland, in November 2001, with the support of the Substance Abuse and Mental Health Services Administration (SAMHSA), issued a report assessing the state of seminary training in the United States.[9] It found that the offerings of today's clergy training institutions vary greatly, with some institutions providing little specific instruction on the subject, and only a few offering complete curricula on addiction. In seminaries accredited by the Association of Theological Schools in the U.S. and Canada, most students enrolled in generalist programs receive little specialized training; at most, an elective course.[10] Reflecting on their own experience, the panelists also noted that the training that is provided may occur too soon, before the clergyperson-in-training has had the life experience to appreciate the need for the information.

The panel recommended that a second panel be convened to develop a set of "core competencies," a listing of the basic knowledge and skills clergy need in order to help addicted individuals and their families. This second panel, which was selected to represent diverse religious perspectives; levels of leadership; and working experience with congregations of diverse socioeconomic status, ethnicity, urban or rural location, and geographical region, met in Washington, D.C., in February 2003. Over the course of a two-day meeting it completed the task of developing the core competencies.[11]

The Structure and Content of the Core Competencies

Because priests have different opportunities in different situations—small vs. large congregations, and adult vs. youth ministries, for example—the core competencies are designed as a general framework which can be expanded upon to apply to different pastoral situations. They reflect the scope and limits of the typical pastoral relationship, and are intended to mesh with the most common spiritual and social goals of such a relationship. Included among these pastoral functions are the following:

- Offering comfort and support to individuals
- Creating communities of mutual caring within parishes
- Educating parishioners and sometimes the larger community about issues of importance to people's well being

The panel outlined the knowledge base that is needed before a priest or other minister can take on the subject of addiction and begin the task of integrating it into his ministry. He or she needs to know something about:

- The neurological mechanisms and behavioral manifestations of the disease
- Its effect on cognitive functioning
- How alcohol or drugs function in the addicted individual's life
- The various environmental harms to families, workplaces, and society as a whole
- The experience of alcohol and other drug dependence—how the disorder affects the "inner world" of the addicted individual and family members

Panelists suggested that a minister should also be able to articulate a "theological anthropology" of addiction; an explanation, in the terms of the particular faith tradition, of how it is a barrier to spirituality and of how recovery can be achieved. The tradition's texts and liturgical practices can serve as resources.

The core competencies are not just elements of knowledge; they are better described as elements of "know how." The panel concluded that, once appropriately trained, pastoral ministers would know how to:

- *Show up.* They would be alert to "windows of opportunity" for contact, assessment, intervention, and treatment.
- *Be dressed.* They would be "prepared internally" with necessary information, resources, and teaching tools.
- *Get through the door.* They would know how to establish effective healing relationships with those affected by addiction.
- *Stay in the boat.* They would do more than hand people off to treatment; they would establish a therapeutic alliance with professionals, congregational caregivers, and the affected individuals and their families.
- *Know when to leave.* They would respect appropriate boundaries and know when to bring their involvement to a conclusion.

These elements of knowledge and practical skills are spelled out in the finished set of twelve core competencies.

> ## "A first step is to bring them to the attention of leaders in seminary training..."

Next Steps

NACoA is working with leaders of multiple denominations and pastoral counseling organizations to disseminate the core competencies widely in faith communities. A first step is to bring them to the attention of leaders in seminary training, and to foster conversations about what should be taught and how it can be fitted into the curriculum. A curriculum development effort has begun, including both pre-ordination and continuing education components. Educational tools will also be developed, including the following:

- A pastoral care outline, giving advice to pastors on when, how, and how extensively to intervene with addicted individuals and their families; how to identify and evaluate community resources; and how to reintegrate the recovering addict into the community
- A preaching and teaching guide, with sample sermons and appropriate religious texts
- A bibliography of resources on addiction and spirituality
- Online courses specifically to teach the lessons implicit in the core competencies

A nationwide "mentors" and "fellows" program is also envisioned. In each major denomination a "mentor" would be identified, who could guide professors in that denomination in their efforts to develop programs or courses. In each seminary there would be a "fellow" who would be responsible for developing such a program or course. Multi-year stipends would be considered.

Conclusion

Faith communities, in their various forms and practices, always have been called on to care for the sick and impaired. The functions of healing, guiding, sustaining, and reconciling are historic and deeply embedded forms of ministry, and they are extremely relevant to parish ministry today. Addictive disorders are clearly evident within parish communities just as they are outside of them, and those who are addicted to alcohol and drugs, and their families and children, need to be able to find pastoral caregivers who are knowledgeable and equipped for this ministry. It is the goal of this Clergy Education and Training Project to make it more likely that their needs will be met.

Reverend C. Roy Woodruff, Ph.D., is a Certified Pastoral Counselor and Diplomate of the American Association of Pastoral Counselors (AAPC), and a Licensed Professional Counselor in the Commonwealth of Virginia. He retired as executive director of AAPC in June 2003, and now serves as a consultant and adjunct seminary professor. He is a member of the Expert Consensus Panel for the Clergy Training Project and author of *Alcoholism and Christian Experience*, among other publications.

Notes

1. See *Substance Abuse: The Nation's Number One Health Problem,* prepared by the Schneider Institute for Health Policy, Brandeis University, for the Robert Wood Johnson Foundation (Princeton, NJ, February 2001).

2. For a description of the distorted relationships within an alcoholic home, see Claudia Black, Ph.D., M.S.W., *It Will Never Happen to Me,* 2nd edition, revised (Bainbridge, WA: MAC Publishing, 2001).

3. "Children of Addicted Parents: Important Facts" (Rockville, MD: National Association for Children of Alcoholics).

4. Christopher C. Ringwald, *The Soul of Recovery: Uncovering the Spiritual Dimension in the Treatment of Addictions,* (Oxford University Press, 2002).

5. C. Roy Woodruff, *Alcoholism and Christian Experience* (Philadelphia, PA: Westminster Press, 1968).

6. *So Help Me God: Substance Abuse, Religion and Spirituality* (New York: National Center on Addiction and Substance Abuse at Columbia University, 1996).

7. Gerald G. May, *Addiction and Grace* (New York: Harper & Row, 1988).

8. Accompanying statement by Joseph A. Califano, Jr., Chairman and President, CASA, p. ii.

9. "Substance Abuse and the Family: Defining the Role of the Faith Community. Phase I: Clergy Training and Curriculum Development." Report of an Expert Panel Meeting, Baltimore, MD, November 14-15, 2001, prepared by the National Association for Children of Alcoholics for the Center for Substance Abuse Treatment (CSAT), Substance Abuse and Mental Health Services Administration (SAMHSA), U.S. Department of Health and Human Services (DHHS), under Contract No. 01M00873601D.

10. This assessment was made by Daniel O. Aleshire, Ph.D., Executive Director, Association of Theological Schools.

11. "Substance Abuse and the Family: Defining the Role of the Faith Community. Phase II: Core Competencies for Clergy and Other Pastoral Ministers in Addressing Alcohol and Other Drug Dependence and the Impact on Family Members." Report of an Expert Consensus Panel Meeting, Washington, D.C., February 26-27, 2003.

CORE COMPETENCIES FOR CLERGY AND PASTORAL MINISTERS IN ADDRESSING ALCOHOL AND OTHER DRUG DEPENDENCE AND THE IMPACT ON FAMILY MEMBERS

These competencies are presented as a specific guide to the core knowledge, attitude, and skills which are essential to the ability of all clergy and pastoral ministers to meet the needs of persons with alcohol or other drug dependence and their family members.

1. Be aware of the:
   - generally accepted definition of alcohol and other drug dependence
   - societal stigma attached to alcohol and other drug dependence

2. Be knowledgeable about the:
   - signs of alcohol and other drug dependence
   - characteristics of withdrawal
   - effects on the individual and the family
   - characteristics of the stages of recovery

3. Be aware that possible indicators of the disease may include, among others: marital conflict, family violence (physical, emotional, and verbal), suicide, hospitalization, or encounters with the criminal justice system.

4. Understand that addiction erodes and blocks religious and spiritual development; and be able to effectively communicate the importance of spirituality and the practice of religion in recovery, using the Scripture, traditions, and rituals of the faith community.

5. Be aware of the potential benefits of early intervention to the:
   - addicted person
   - family system
   - affected children

6. Be aware of appropriate pastoral interactions with the:
   - addicted person
   - family system
   - affected children

7. Be able to communicate and sustain:
   - an appropriate level of concern
   - messages of hope and caring

8. Be familiar with and utilize available community resources to ensure a continuum of care for the:
   - addicted person
   - family system
   - affected children

9. Have a general knowledge of and, where possible, exposure to:
   - the 12-step programs of AA, NA, Al-Anon, Nar-Anon, Alateen, A.C.O.A., etc.
   - other groups

10. Be able to acknowledge and address values, issues, and attitudes regarding alcohol and other drug use and dependence in:
    - oneself
    - one's own family

11. Be able to shape, form, and educate a caring congregation that welcomes and supports persons and families affected by alcohol and other drug dependence.

12. Be aware of how prevention strategies can benefit the larger community.

(NACoA, 2003)

A Case Study Approach to Teaching Chemical Dependency in Seminary Formation: An Application of the Core Competencies

Reverend Mark A. Latcovich and Sis Wenger

This article is reprinted from Seminary Journal, *Volume 9, Winter 2003.*

CASE #1 — Doing Good Doesn't Mean Things are Good

She had four children, was president of the mothers' club, had been a member of the parish council. She was lovely, kind, helpful, and a devoted wife, mother, and volunteer. And she was dead of alcoholism at age 40. There were many priests on the altar at her funeral. Most knew she had a serious drinking problem and had witnessed it often. They cared about her and her family and treated them kindly and with respect. They didn't know what else to do and didn't want to offend, so they said nothing when the children and other family members said nothing. They cared, but they weren't equipped.

Educational Focus

People are not born knowing how to deal effectively with someone else's addiction. Seldom do family members, friends, or clergy instinctively avoid enabling behaviors and find appropriate ways to intervene. The great majority stumble along managing each day the best they can, repeating what doesn't work. Although this response to alcoholism is normal, it adds to the confusion and suffering of the children involved. It also does not address the underlying issue: A key family member or parishioner is suffering from a chronic, fatal disease and needs intervention and treatment which are frequently highly successful at arresting this disease and establishing the base for lifetime healing and recovery.

> **"Effective intervention strategies are counterintuitive, so they need to be learned."**

Effective intervention strategies are counterintuitive, so they need to be learned. Being supportive and encouraging is a "pastoral" norm. With addiction, addressing the alcohol or drug use firmly and with concern is a critical pastoral role. Being able to articulate, with compassion and knowledge, the consequences of alcohol and drug use for the individual, the family and (where appropriate) the congregation, can make a life-altering impact on an individual or a family. Knowing the benefits of structured family intervention (see sidebar) and where to refer concerned family members for professional assistance can and does save lives and families from the devastation of chronic alcoholism.

CASE #2 — Behind the Marriage Failures

John P. petitioned for an annulment, blaming his wife's irrational and controlling behavior for the collapse of their marriage. He had been a drinking alcoholic for the whole of their ten years of marriage, and there were three children ages four through eight.

Educational Focus

The majority of spouses of alcoholics are not irrational, mentally ill, or control freaks. They are simply overwhelmed by the insanity of someone else's addiction. Often they are reliving the nightmare of their own childhood, growing up in the chaos caused by a parent's drinking; feeling as helpless, confused, and frightened as adults as they did when they were children. Spouses of those addicted to alcohol or drugs need clarity about the disease that is crushing their lives and family. They need support offered

> ## "They need to hear messages of hope and the possibility of recovery for their whole family, and they need help in finding the resources they need."

by such groups as Al-Anon. They need to hear messages of hope and the possibility of recovery for their whole family, and they need help in finding the resources they need.

These messages of hope and healing must come from outside the family, preferably from a trusted source of care and support. In the faith community, these messages can come from posters in the halls; pamphlets in the racks; information in the parish bulletin; and Alcoholics Anonymous, Al-Anon or Alateen meetings on church property with the times listed in the bulletin. They can come from statements included in the homilies that describe the pervasiveness of the disease, making it clear that the only shame in this disease is doing nothing to help.

INTERVENTION WORKS

Intervention is a process which attempts to crack the delusion in which alcoholic/addicted people live. It is the delusion that keeps addicted persons in denial about their disease and its consequences—for themselves and for their loved ones. Intervention works because it punctures the delusion.

Intervention gathers together the people who:
- care most about the individual;
- have detailed information/facts which show that the person is in trouble; and
- are able to express love, concern, and a genuine desire for re-connection along with the stark facts of the disease's impact.

The caring and facts presented together (neither alone) are what puts cracks in the delusion. While addicted individuals are brilliant at staying in denial if the concern and facts are presented on a one-to-one basis, it becomes too overwhelming to counteract when presented all at once in a group setting where it is clear that the people most important to them are united. When it all comes at once, the delusion begins to crumble, and the love and reality begin to set in.

The interventionist (a trained professional) is there to help the addicted person's loved ones express their concerns and state the facts in a "receivable" form. Prior to the intervention meeting, the interventionist educates the family and other concerned participants, helps them to organize the intervention and what will be presented, guides them to understand their own options for healing, and assists in determining and arranging for the most appropriate treatment for the addicted family member. Most people will accept treatment on the day of the intervention.

Trained intervention specialists who are skilled in family therapy as well as the techniques of conducting an intervention can be found in most communities. Hazelden (1-800-328-9000 or www.hazelden.org) has two books on intervention: a landmark book, *Intervention: How to Help Someone Who Doesn't Want Help*, and *Love First: A New Approach to Intervention for Alcoholism and Drug Addiction*. National sources for locating interventionists nationwide are: the Association of Intervention Specialists (301-670-2800) and the Intervention Resource Center (1-888-421-4321).

Core Competencies for Clergy and Other Pastoral Ministers in Addressing Alcohol and Drug Dependence and the Impact on Family Members was developed by a multi-denominational expert consensus panel of Faith and Seminary leaders. The effort was supported by the Substance Abuse and Mental Health Services Administration (SAMHSA), U.S. Department of Health and Human Services.

For free copies of the full document, contact SAMHSA's clearinghouse at 1-800-729-6686 or online at www.samhsa.gov or www.nacoa.org

For information on the Clergy Education and Training Project contact:

National Association for Children of Alcoholics
Telephone: 301-468-0985
E-mail: nacoa@nacoa.org

Preparing Clergy to Serve Families Facing Chemical Dependency

The annulment was granted, but before another marriage could be attempted, the husband was required to be certified "sober" for a year by a Tribunal-designated psychologist. He drank the whole year, but seldom appeared intoxicated. He was declared "sober" and cleared to marry. Less than three years later, the second wife left him because of his alcoholism.

The Diocesan Marriage Tribunal typically is a careful and caring investigative body, working to preserve the sanctity of the sacrament while acknowledging that a given marriage may never have existed in certain circumstances. What this Tribunal missed was the "main event" for the petitioner, his wives, and his children: Alcoholism was calling the shots, and the spouse's response was "normal" for the situation. The disease needed to be addressed first as potentially causal for all presenting issues. The petitioner needed treatment; both wives and the children needed therapy and/or 12-step support services. The whole family was suffering from this disease, and everyone needed to recover—even the young children. Members of a Marriage Tribunal, however, cannot ask the requisite questions that will surface these needs when it does not have the basic knowledge and skills essential to do so.

CASE #3 — The Missed Topic in Marriage Preparation

It was a casual comment to a professional colleague who helped with the new marriage preparation programs in her diocese. "I wonder how many divorces we'd have prevented if we had included a session on alcoholism, other drug use problems, and the impact on adults of having grown up in an alcoholic family." The colleague said she knew because she had instituted such a program in her diocese. In the first year, she reported, a half-day was added covering the nature of alcoholism, its signs and symptoms for the addicted person and for family members, its progression, and the negative consequences (often life-long if not addressed) of growing up in an affected family. After the educational session, 20% of the couples decided not to marry, or to postpone marriage until counseling was obtained for the unresolved childhood issues of being an adult child of an alcoholic parent or until one partner addressed his or her excessive drinking. After adequate treatment or counseling, about 25% returned to prepare for marriage.

Educational Focus

When one in four children under 18—across all economic, social, religious, and cultural groups—lives in a family with alcohol abuse or alcoholism, and countless others suffer because of parental drug use, it is crucial that clergy and other pastoral ministers have a clear understanding of addiction's effect on the physical, emotional, and spiritual well-being of their parish families.

It is widely known that this disease, if untreated, destroys marriages and alienates families from their church. Not only does alcoholism block the capacity for a meaningful

> ## "It is crucial that clergy and other pastoral ministers have a clear understanding of addiction's effect..."

spiritual life, it blocks the capacity for healthy, appropriate, interpersonal relationships and partnerships. Both engaged couples and their parishes would benefit from assuring that those who present themselves for the sacrament of marriage are actually capable of entering into and sustaining a sacramental partnership over a lifetime.

CASE #4 — Mother's Day, Father's Day, and So Much Pain

It was Mothers' Day many years ago, and she had just returned from Sunday Mass. She called her mentor to say, "I remembered again this morning why I hated to go to church on Mother's Day—because I had to listen to another sermon extolling mothers and the sacrifices they make for their families. All I could remember was her drunken rages, putting her to bed at night while my executive father "worked" in his library, and hiding in the attic in order to study for exams. I don't want to be like her, and I don't want to attend Mass with my children on Mothers' Day and listen to what is a lie for too many children."

Educational Focus

When addiction is present, the "no talk" rules impede or block expressions of pain, fear, anger, and confusion. Consequently, these feelings don't get processed and worked through in healthy ways. The rule of silence about the family's "truth" is coupled with rigid expectations of "looking good" behavior, creating barriers to seeking help.

What would it take to add a note to that Mother's Day sermon, asking parishioners to pray for those mothers who would like to live up to the ideal that has just been discussed but are trapped in alcohol or drug addiction—or in mental illness—and cannot be what their children need without outside help. Or add to the prayers of the faithful a prayer that these mothers and their families be guided into treatment and recovery soon, that children living in the confusion and fear created by alcohol or drug use in their families will find safe and supportive adults to whom they can turn.

CASE #5 — The Clergy as Counselors

She is the mother of five. She came to seek help for her husband's drinking from the parish priest, whom her husband liked and admired, who was also a psychologist. She was reminded that her husband is a nice person and advised that she should be less critical and give him more support. She found Al-Anon, which saved her sanity, but her marriage ended. She raised the five children while he found a younger woman who was willing to tolerate his drunken behavior. The priest did care—about the husband, the wife, and the children—but his graduate training did not include adequate information on alcoholism, its impact on family members, especially developing children, and how to

RESOURCES FOR SEMINARY OR PARISH LIBRARIES

Ackerman, Robert. *Silent Sons.* Simon & Schuster, 1993.

Black, Claudia. *It Will Never Happen To Me.* Ballantine Books, 1987.

Johnson, Vernon, Johnson Institute. *Intervention: How To Help Someone Who Doesn't Want Help.* Hazelden, 1986.

Jay, Jeff and Debra. *Love First: A New Approach to Intervention for Alcoholism and Drug Addiction.* Hazelden, 2000.

Ketchum, Katherine; Arthur Ciaramicoli; Mel Schulstad; and William Asbury. *Beyond the Influence: Understanding and Defeating Alcoholism.* Bantam, 2000.

Wholey, Dennis. *Courage to Change.* Mass Market Paperback, 1994.

Helpful Web sites

Alcoholics Anonymous: www.aa.org

Al-Anon and Alateen: www.al-anon.org

Adult Children of Alcoholics: www.adultchildren.org

Co-Dependents Anonymous: www.codependents.org

Johnson Institute: www.johnsoninstitute.org

National Association for Children of Alcoholics: www.nacoa.org

National Center on Addiction and Substance Abuse at Columbia University: www.casacolumbia.org

National Council on Alcoholism and Drug Dependency: www.ncadd.org

National Clearinghouse for Alcohol and Drug Information: www.ncadi.samhsa.gov

help intervene and break the cycle of family confusion and pain. He didn't understand that, when he visited the family, the children hoped he would notice, say something, do something to help. They were his friends and he cared deeply about them. But he didn't understand their silence or how to break the "no talk" rule that trapped them all.

Educational Focus

Hurting parishioners generally perceive clergy and pastoral ministers as potential sources of help and support. Parishioners may present with "marriage problems" or "unfaithfulness" and often do not name the alcohol or drug use as the culprit. Frequently, people who live with addiction do not recognize it for what it is—a chronic, debilitating disease that will get worse over time unless interrupted.

Clergy are seldom prepared to deal with addiction-related issues, yet those issues will affect the counseling and many decisions they will address throughout their priesthood. A survey (*So Help Me God!*) released by the Center on Addiction and Substance Abuse at Columbia University in November, 1999, reported that 94.4% of clergy considered addiction to be an important issue they confronted, yet only 12.5% had done any course work on it during their seminary studies. This begs the question: How can clergy attain the knowledge and skills necessary to be effective in addressing alcoholism and other drug dependencies in afflicted individuals and their affected family members? The "Core Competencies for Clergy and Other Pastoral Ministers In Addressing Alcohol and Other Drug Dependence and the Impact on Family Members" discussed by Reverend Roy C. Woodruff, Ph.D., elsewhere in this issue establish the basis for appropriate educational modules that can be incorporated into existing courses and post-ordination educational programs. We have waited too long and watched too many of our Catholic families crumble under the destructive power of alcoholism, affecting generation after generation. We must find a way to equip our present and future clergy to address this disease effectively.

Children of alcohol or drug dependent parents need a safe haven where they can meet

> ## "But he didn't understand their silence or how to break the 'no talk' rule that trapped them all."

adults who will talk to them openly about what may have been their "family secret." The isolation and stigma the children may feel are lifted when trusted adults validate their experience, and when they learn that others face the same confusion and chaos that dominates their lives. When those "trusted adults" are part of their parish leadership, they gain hope and become free to pursue a spiritual connectedness with God and to feel that they can "belong" and be valued in the parish community. When they learn they are not responsible for what is happening in their families, that they are not alone, and that their parish community, especially its leadership, recognizes their intrinsic worth, children can be empowered to make healthy choices for themselves, with the support of their faith community.

Most parishes have members who are knowledgeable about addiction and recovery and are willing to join an effort to identify and support both those who are afflicted and their family members. Faith Partners, a congregational team-approach program offered by the Johnson Institute's Rush Center in Austin, Texas, takes advantage of that pool of resources to create an education and support team at the parish level. This effective program has spread to several hundred faith communities across the country, including many Catholic parishes. A Faith Partners team of professionals and concerned persons—including some recovering alcoholics or family members as well as health and addiction treatment professionals—is pulled together from within the parish and approved by the pastor and parish council. The team surveys parish members about their concerns and services needed. It then crafts the initial solutions to meet the perceived needs of the parish. It provides educational programs, reading materials, referrals, and acts as the source to which concerned persons, including the parish leadership, can come for guidance and information about alcohol and drug-related issues.

The team can play a unique role in helping troubled family members seeking guidance about a loved one's drinking or drug use, in supporting early intervention, and in recovery support for both parishioners who have entered treatment for addiction and for their families. This approach gives maximum help to parishioners suffering the consequences of addiction and their family members; yet it does not require the already-overburdened pastor to take on an additional responsibility. For more information, visit www.rushcenter.org.

> **"Their picture of God may be the image of an abusive father, a codependent mother, or a parent that has abandoned them."**

Application of the Core Competencies to the Seminary Curriculum

Each of these scenarios could be used as a case study as part of a course in pastoral counseling or to stimulate discussion at an in-service day on alcoholism and substance abuse. They warrant a critical review by seminary students who need to be exposed to the complexities and nuances of addiction. Seminary curriculum dealing with addictions usually teaches students how to refer and utilize community resources. However, seminaries also must remind the seminarians to develop a pastoral instinct that comes from integrating skills with personal formation. When seminaries teach these future pastors to follow their gut reactions and trust the spiritual traditions of the faith community, the competencies they learn become part of the healing ministry of the church.

Substance abuse and addiction is a systemic deconstruction that estranges, alienates, and sedates the self from God. Ministers who support individuals in treatment need to be ready to offer some guidance, especially after treatment. The aftercare process of recovery often includes the need to forgive oneself. It involves a reconciling community that invites those who have been estranged from each other to rediscover each other and themselves all over again. This process of healing is often initiated within a parish community through the assistance of a priest or pastoral minister who serves as a spiritual mentor. This mentor in faith reformation needs to be attentive to the faulty images of God the persons in recovery have constructed. Their picture of God may be the image of an abusive father, a codependent mother, or a parent that has abandoned them. The person in recovery may be overcompensating with rigid behaviors and beliefs or have little or no religious formation. As individuals reengage intrinsic support systems, they may need some pastoral assistance in clarifying their faith connections. They may need to feel the welcoming hands of a faith community that provides patience, understanding, and acceptance. The priest can help the person in recovery rebuild a biblical and theological anthropology that includes a God who forgives.

One's self-image throughout addiction is poor. Helping individuals appreciate the Christian perspective of a saved and redeemed humanity is essential for recovery and healing. Seminarians that can link their systematic theology courses with the art of pastoral healing may one day be priests that provide spiritual guidance for individuals who have lived in tangled relationships with shattered hopes. As future priests, seminarians will constantly invite people to be members of a faith community. They will need to assist those who have lost meaning for their life. Furthermore, ongoing ministry is needed to help individuals reshape feelings of guilt or resentment into self-forgiveness and a positive self-love. The future ministers would do well to appreciate that they possess a reservoir of lived faith and always have access to a religious tradition that is firmly rooted in reconciliation, contrition, and conversion. This delicate and complex process of recovery is a process that demands patience, gentleness, understanding, and sympathy.

Seminarians at one point or another in their curriculum should understand the dynamics of Alcoholics Anonymous, especially the Fifth Step Process (see The Clergyperson and the Fifth Step in Robert J Kus, ed., 1995, *Spirituality and Chemical Dependency*. The Haworth Press). Students need to appreciate the importance of support groups during recovery. The seminary internship year affords many opportunities to become acquainted with various support groups. Students in their pastoral year could interview and visit local agencies that support addiction recovery. The personalization that comes from meeting a sponsor in an "Alcoholics Anonymous" or "Al-Anon" support group, or a meeting with a counselor who organizes family interventions helps shape the mind and heart with hands-on learning that can later serve as a valuable resource.

Conclusion

The "Core Competencies for Clergy" provide a framework for acquiring the knowledge and skills needed in each of these case studies. In Case #2, for example, core competencies #1, 2, 3, 6, and 9 would have provided the parish priest an opportunity to offer support and guidance to the spouse and children, while helping to intervene and refer the alcoholic to treatment.°In this way, the priest could be instrumental in a family's healing process and return to emotional stability. The priest's actions would also offer to the family members a renewed capacity to connect with their spiritual roots.

Mastering the Core Competencies can help prepare the seminary student to develop a healthy attitude about alcohol use, the impact it might have had on his own life, and the ability to reach out and support the many individuals and families in their parishes affected by alcohol or drug dependence.

Reverend Mark A. Latcovich, Ph.D., is vice rector and academic dean at Saint Mary Seminary and Graduate School of Theology, Wickliffe, Ohio. He received his Ph.D. from Case Western Reserve University, Cleveland, Ohio.

Sis Wenger is the executive director of the National Association for Children of Alcoholics (NACoA). She was an adjunct associate professor in addictions studies at the University of Detroit Mercy in Detroit, Michigan, for over ten years. She is a member of the President's Advisory Commission on Drug Free Communities. Sis has received numerous honors for her professional and volunteer work in the field of addictions and family, including two presidential awards.

Psychospirituality of Addiction

Kevin P. McClone, M.Div., Psy.D.

This article is reprinted from Seminary Journal, *Volume 9, Winter 2003.*

Introduction

I am grateful to respond to the invitation to offer some critical reflections on the psychospirituality of addiction. My reflections in this article come in large part from a presentation I made to the regional Illinois Alcohol and Other Drug Abuse Professional Certification Association (IAODAPCA) Spring Conference held March 25, 2002, as well as insights from the theological students I have taught in a course titled "Ministry to Persons and Families Struggling with Addictions" at Catholic Theological Union in Chicago.

Multiple scientific studies and research have concluded that addictions are complex illnesses with a wide variety of interacting factors coming into play. No one factor or cause has been determined. Nevertheless, one crucial aspect that is often neglected is the interaction of psychological and spiritual factors in our understanding of addictions. In this paper, I will examine the pervasive nature of addictions in our world and highlight the soul sickness that underlies the addictive process. After examining the nature and extent of addictions as soul sickness, I will explore several psychospiritual issues that underlie the dynamics of addiction that may help pave the way to more effective recovery and relapse prevention.

The Problem

I would venture to say that whether or not we are struggling with an addiction or compulsive behavior, we probably have been touched personally by addictions because of their prevalence in our families, society, and wider culture. So too, a growing concern in seminaries and among priests and religious men and women is the impact of addiction in our families, communities, and church. As Howard Clinebell noted in his book *Understanding and Counseling Persons with Alcohol, Drug, and Behavioral Addictions,* "Addictions constitute one of the most widespread and costly problems of contemporary society. Indeed it is a rare person or family whose life has not been impacted directly or indirectly by some addiction."

In this technological age, addictions are growing at a phenomenal rate. We live in a modern age of rapid change and technological advances that promise relief, happiness, and satisfaction for life's many hungers. It is a culture that actively promotes pain avoidance. In our fast-paced world we have little time to reflect on our lives or to be with friends and family. We consume more and more but taste less. We buy more goods and yet are left wanting more. According to research by Patrick Carnes, one of the fastest growing addictions today is cybersex and other Internet addictions. In my own counseling, I see more and more children and adults impacted by addictions of various sorts. The cover story in the June 2001 issue of the American Psychological Association's magazine, the *Monitor,* was on addiction. This article reported that drug, alcohol, and tobacco use is the cause of more deaths, illnesses, and disabilities than any other preventable health condition and seriously undermines America's family life, economy, and public safety.

Many of the students in my addiction course at Catholic Theological Union come from countries outside the United States. They have reminded me of how much the knowledge and awareness of addictions is important for their future ministry and pastoral work. For one student from Kenya, it was concern for the epidemic problem of sniffing glue by street children. For another student from Mexico, cocaine addiction and drug trafficking were a key pastoral issue. Whether here in the U.S. or abroad, addictions present a worldwide problem of devastating proportions.

Whatever the experience, we seem to live in a world in which there is no shortage of compulsive and addictive behaviors. Indeed, ministry to persons and families who struggle with addictions is a crucial need in the church today and one that continues to grow as new forms of addiction are added to the mix. There is a fast-growing community of recovering persons in a variety of twelve-step groups throughout the United States and abroad. All ministers would benefit, it seems, from knowing more about the dynamics of these various addictions, especially from a psychospiritual perspective, and how to best minister to the thousands of persons and families affected.

> **"The spirituality of addiction is a spirituality of possession where the person has no real being or is a lost soul..."**

Lost Souls

The spirituality of addiction is a spirituality of possession where the person has no real being or is a lost soul, disconnected from self, others, and God in a profound way. Indeed, if we trace the origins of addiction, we see that the word addicted comes from the Latin prefix *ad*, which means "to" or "forward," and the past participle *dicere*, which means to "say" or "pronounce." This old notion meant a formal giving over or

delivery by a sentence of the court, such as when surrendered to or obligated to a master. Though this more formal legal sense drops out of contemporary usage, still, the addict in a very real sense is someone who is delivered over to a master. Gerald May in his book *Addiction and Grace* describes addictions and compulsions as enslavements. Psychologically, May states that addiction uses up desire, sucking life energy into specific obsessions and compulsions, leaving less energy for other people and pursuits.

In my own work with persons struggling with various addictions, I have seen first hand the real loss of freedom as the addictive substance or behavior claims possession of their time, their thoughts, and their relationships. Clearly, they lose their sense of freedom and in a real way are claimed by the objects of their addictions. So through their own acts, addicts *ad-dict* themselves, they cease to become one's own. They are left feeling restless, frightened, insecure, self-centered, anxious, and psychologically and spiritually bankrupt.

Harold Doweiko, a psychologist who has worked for many years in the addiction recovery field, has indicated that substance abuse disorders are symptoms of a spiritual disease and remind us that the Greek word for the soul, *psyche*, is the root of the word, psychotherapy. So with regard to addiction, in a very real sense we can speak of psychospiritual recovery from addiction as involving soul therapy. Crucial to the addiction recovery process is the integrating of psychological insights into a program of recovery that fosters the person's spiritual growth.

Misdirected Spiritual Search

Carl Jung stated that craving for alcohol was really a search for wholeness or union with God. The Latin term for alcohol is *spiritus* and, he remarked, "You use the same word for the highest religious experience as well as for the most depraving poison." Addictions often have been viewed in such existential and spiritual language, as Lee Jampolsky so aptly notes: "Addiction is fundamentally a misdirected spiritual search that is rooted in a fundamental belief that I am not OK the way I am and there is a void that needs to be filled and something external to myself will fill this void."

Victor Frankl concluded that substance abuse might be a response to a loss of direction within the individual. It is a spiritual search for peace in a world of restless anxiety. The alcohol, drug, work, or sexual behavior provides a temporary sense of relief and feeling of control that the addict desperately seeks. The addiction tells us we can have it now, a message reinforced in the wider culture in a wide variety of ways every day. Howard Clinebell notes that the insecurity and emotional malnutrition bred by an anxious, violent, and competitive society has resulted in many damaged orphans of the spirit. Bill Wilson, one of the cofounders of Alcoholics Anonymous, referred to alcoholism as a soul sickness or a form of spiritual bankruptcy.

One way that twelve-step recovery speaks of spirituality is getting out of oneself and beginning to order one's life in relationship to a higher power. Sandra Schneider captures this fundamental understanding when she (1986, 1990) describes spirituality as the "experience of consciously striving to integrate one's life in terms of self-transcendence toward the ultimate value one perceives." Addiction is one state of being, albeit misguided, that also seeks meaning, peace, and transcendence. Addiction is misguided because it seeks to replace God with objects or attachments that command our allegiance. At the heart of the addictive process is a restless spirit that is seeking answers but has set off in the wrong direction. The path is an outer-directed search that denies one's true self while caught in the web of idolatry and self-deception. Indeed, denial is the hallmark of the addictive process.

The problem with addictions is that they seem to work, at least for awhile, for many persons. What do you mean they work? How could something so destructive to the person, family, and friends being seen as working? By seeming to work, I mean that there is a reward, a payoff, a benefit, a way to deal with life's stresses, pain, and unpredictability. Recently, a client of mine shared how he knew that alcohol was destroying his life but yet was convinced he couldn't imagine a world without alcohol. Alcohol had been his most reliable friend. As someone fearful of intimacy and very lonely, alcohol allowed him to feel like one of group and even the life of the party.

> **"I have seen first hand the real loss of freedom as the addictive substance or behavior claims possession..."**

Those who struggle with compulsive and addictive patterns often will describe their addictive substance or behavior in relational language such as "Alcohol was my friend," or "I could always rely on this drug to be there for me." Caroline Knapp in her autobiographical account of her addiction to alcohol describes her drinking as a "love story." "Yes; this is a love story...I loved the way drink made me feel, and I loved its special power of deflection, its ability to shift my focus away from my own awareness of self and onto something else, something less painful than my own feelings." She goes on to talk about her love affair and relationship with alcohol that grew gradually through the years until it became a central part of who she was.

Compulsive use of alcohol, drugs, sex, gambling, work, or the Internet may all serve as a temporary solution to feelings of shame, loneliness, depression, or hurt feelings. However, the paradox of addictions is that the more we seek relief, the more we find misery, and the more we are fed, the more hunger we feel. Augustine put it well when he said that our hearts are restless, until they rest in Thee. The search for peace, relief, and contentment in drugs, alcohol, food, work, sex, and the Internet provide a false temporary escape that masks the real dilemma of the empty lost soul within. These disordered attachments are none the less attachments. They seek to fill a need or void deep within us but ultimately leave us spiritually empty.

My belief is that we cannot fully understand the road to recovery until we see that these addictions and over dependencies serve a deep need that is still unmet in the person. This need at root is deeply psychospiritual. The problem is that with addictions the person regresses often to a more childlike state of maturity in this false or misdirected search for the transcendent. Sober life demands far too much for immature persons, and they may often be tempted to relapse where the demands are minimal and pleasure is injected quicker. The challenge for men and women of faith is to offer a countercultural message of peace and serenity through a radically different approach. A message that is too often unproclaimed is that real joy is in the long, bumpy, and winding road!

> ## "The challenge for men and women of faith is to offer a countercultural message of peace and serenity through a radically different approach."

The Road to Psychospiritual Recovery

Now that we have explored the nature of the problem, I would like to propose some psychospiritual issues that may help guide the recovery process along the long and bumpy road for the recovering addict and those affected by addictive systems.

1. From a Lack of Conscious Awareness to a Spiritual Awakening and Living Consciously in the Now

One of the great spiritual truths is that awareness in the present moment allows us a glimpse of eternity. We can race through life or seek refuge in all sorts of false comforts, but ultimately some of life's deepest treasures are found in the presence to life, whether a sunset, a friend's support, or the play of a child. Most of these gifts can be lost, not because they don't exist in our world but for failing to notice them. I recall one recovering person telling me, "Its amazing how I can just enjoy the little things of life today." This person went on to describe how these miracles were always there, but he was blinded by the restless anxiety of his compulsive drinking and unable to see what was always so near. It is the addict's preoccupation with the past and the future that blocks awareness and

responsiveness in the present moment. Conscious living in the now allows one to live life on its own terms. It means that one feels pain and fear but also joy and serenity.

Living consciously allows us to actively and creatively participate in the beauty and sorrows of life without the cloud of substances that would dull our experience. Ultimately, this greater awareness can lead to a gradual spiritual awakening. Indeed, twelve-step movements began with the first drunk having an awakening through a profound "spiritual experience" while detoxifying at Towns Hospital. Later Bill Wilson's conversation of shared pain and shared hope with another alcoholic, Dr. Bob, eventually led to the journey of recovery for millions of alcoholics worldwide. In the *Big Book* of Alcoholics Anonymous, Bill Wilson highlights the spiritual solution that has led to personal transformation in these words:

> The great fact is just this, and nothing less: That we have had deep and effective spiritual experiences which have revolutionized our whole attitude toward life, toward our fellows, and toward God's universe. (p. 25)

The psychospiritual journey and the search for meaning involve a revolutionary new way of seeing oneself, others, and one's higher power. Addicts seek pleasure in substances and activities outside of themselves and fear solitude and contemplation, which only confronts them with their emptiness within. Psychospiritual recovery involves coming to a radical new awareness that allows one to live more fully in the now.

2. From Self-Deception and Control to Humility and Letting Go

Control is often rooted in my inability to accept myself as I am, and the more insecure I feel, the more I need to control my world. Patrick Carnes in his research on sexual addiction notes that one of the primary beliefs of the sexual addict is that no one could possible love me for who I am. Rather than confront these feelings of shame and self-loathing, the addict instead engages in a spiraling down cycle of preoccupation with his addictive behavior that only leads to

> **"The psychospiritual journey and the search for meaning involve a revolutionary new way of seeing oneself, others, and one's higher power."**

further shame and low self-worth. Denial and self-centeredness are two hallmarks of the addictive process. For the addict, this often leads to a double life, or a Jekyll and Hyde existence, and a world surrounded in fear and hiding from the light of truth.

Being honest is one of the most difficult things for a life built on denial. These psychological defenses, whether denial, rationalization, or projection, are aimed at protecting underlying feelings of inferiority, fear, guilt, and shame. The individual addict uses substances or behaviors to numb or narcotize internal pain and attempts to force their will on the universe. The individual who is focused on self-centered needs wants what he wants when he wants it. Bill Wilson aptly notes in the *Big Book* of AA, "Selfishness and self-centeredness…is the root of our troubles and…driven by a hundred forms of fear, self-delusion, self-seeking, and self pity, we step on the toes of our fellows and they retaliate" (p. 62). Substances provide an escape by giving us feelings of self-confidence and the illusion of strength and may have tremendous appeal to those who are submerged in powerlessness, shame, disappointment, frustration, and self-rejection.

Psychospiritual recovery involves bringing the light of truth to shine on the mask, persona, and false self the individual addict hides behind. The acceptance one feels in twelve-step recovery groups often provides such an opportunity. Early in recovery the addict's resistance is often at its peak, and that is why most relapses occur within the first six months of sobriety. But gradually through asking for help and attending twelve-step meetings, the recovering person realizes he or she need not go it alone and finds it easier to surrender the tight grasp of control.

Humility is recognizing our fundamental need for others and God. The addict no longer feels the need to be at the center of the universe but becomes one among the many. This in turn allows him to move out of self-centered fear and reliance on self to reliance on others and his higher power. He or she in turn is able to become more compassionate with his or her own limitations. Humility is not thinking too much or too little of oneself but a more realistic acceptance of who we are with all our strengths and limitations.

3. From Fear to Trust

What often holds the addict off from seeking help is not necessarily that they feel life is going well, although denial may allow such masking for awhile. The deeper reality may be that it is frightening to imagine what life would be like without their addiction of choice. For those struggling with compulsions and addictions, fear and anxiety are intolerable realities that must be avoided rather than the normal realties of living in a world of loss, change, and ambiguity. The alcohol, drug, work, food, gambling, addictive relationship, or Internet addiction all tend to numb our awareness of these anxieties and tensions.

What is missing is the courage to face one's fears openly. Recovery involves gradually coming to face both one's fears and life on life's terms. In other words, to recognize that to be human is to live embracing one's fears but without despair. Fear is a natural human experience, and the need for a basic trust in the universe is never outgrown. However, it becomes apparent that doubt, despair, and disillusionment combine to make the individual vulnerable to temptations offered by anything that seeks to ease the suffering. The root of despair is in the need for control or security. The addict fears surrender to an absolute or higher power as a loss of control of having his or her own way.

One recovering alcoholic stated that he never could relax in his own skin and was always running, restless and unsettled. Many of those who struggle with addictions have described this profound state of alienation from themselves and others. The restlessness is partially rooted in the fear of facing oneself honestly. To confront the illusionary self in the mirror of truth can be a terrifying experience for the compulsive or addicted person.

Psychospiritual recovery is the movement out of being lost, isolated, alone, afraid, and without meaning and purpose, to an inner-directed hopeful search for serenity and peace rooted in the best spiritual principles of love, community, and intimacy with self, God, others, and nature. One gradually discovers he or she is no longer disconnected, fearful, and restless but aware that life is precious, and each moment brings the potential for deeper spiritual awakenings.

4. Immediate Gratification versus Healthy Asceticism

Fulfillment paradoxically comes through healthy asceticism, sacrifice, and surrender. It comes not from seeking more but by being at peaceful and content with less. The more we fill ourselves, the more we take, the more empty we become. Discipline is feared by the person struggling with an addiction, and self-centeredness and impulsive behaviors are often seen as hallmarks of the addictive process.

In spiritual traditions, human attempts to receive and respond to grace are called asceticism. The word comes from the Greek *askeo*, "to exercise." It refers to all authentic intentions and efforts we make toward fulfilling our deepest desires for God. Asceticism, according to Gerald May, is our willingness to enter into the deserts of our lives, to commit ourselves to the struggle with attachment, to participate in a courtship with grace. We need God's grace to help us through the deserts of addictions. Discipline and asceticism get a bad rap, but the truth is healthy discipline makes us freer.

Psychospiritual recovery involves a radical shift in perception that begins to see self-discipline and healthy asceticism as essential on the road to true and more lasting peace and serenity. This spiritual message has been at the heart of the world's great religious and spiritual traditions.

5. Perfectionism versus Acceptance of Limitations

False pride often can become a wall behind which the addict hides. It is necessary to give up the search for perfection. Spirituality is less about getting it right all the time and more about realizing that pain, struggle, and mistakes are an

> **"Psychospiritual recovery is the movement out of being lost, isolated, alone, afraid, and without meaning and purpose, to an inner-directed hopeful search for serenity and peace rooted in the best spiritual principles of love, community, and intimacy with self, God, others, and nature."**

essential part of living. Ernest Kurtz and Katherine Ketchum, in their book *The Spirituality of Imperfection*, use the analogy of baseball to remind us that like baseball, errors are part of the game of life. Unfortunately, perfection has lost its real meaning. The real meaning of perfection is wholeness or to be complete or whole. To be whole is to accept one's own limitations as well as strengths. At the heart of the spirituality of the twelve steps is a genuine acceptance and acknowledgment of one's strengths and weaknesses.

What has eluded the addict is that false notions of perfection have led to hard inner judgments, shame, and never feeling good enough. Lewis Presnall, in his classic book *The Search for Serenity*, states, "No one can be at home in his own heaven until he has learned to be at home in his own hell." The full appreciation of inner serenity is achieved only after having to come to terms with one's own weakness, limitations, and shortcomings. Indeed, the sixth and seventh steps of the twelve steps of AA deal precisely with the psychospiritual process of owning one's shortcomings and humbly asking God to remove them.

6. From Never Enough to Gratitude

Lee Jampolsky, in his article "Healing the Addictive Mind," notes that scarcity is a predominant belief in American society that we are always lacking something. This addictive philosophy of "not enough" leads us into endless pursuits to fill this perceived void. Much of our emotional pain comes from what we feel we lack, so we search for endless relationships to fill the void. The media reflect this idea to us in countless commercials that tell us what product will help fill the emptiness and make us whole. One of the telltale signs of early recovery from addiction is that the addict begins to speak more from a heart of gratitude than scarcity. Gratitude is a fundamental awareness that one has received a gift, and this radical change in perception is a filter that begins to shape one's experiences in later recovery. One person in recovery for years put it this way: "If it never gets any better than this, I will take it." It's the secret of learning real acceptance and gratitude despite the ups and downs life may bring. It is the story of the prodigal son or other biblical narratives of mercy that depict the experience of radical transformation when one feels a part of the human community again.

Whenever I meet or work with recovering persons who seem to being doing well, I'm struck by the gratitude that seems to well up from within them. It seems to flow out of a center rooted in one who is deeply aware of a profound gift. It doesn't seem that the gratitude is tied to material riches, although life for many addicts may indeed improve financially in recovery, but rather in a transformed perspective on life that gives them a new vision for living. Recovery in addiction is all about a radical shift in perception that allows seeing what before was blind to us, as the hymn Amazing Grace points out. The grateful recovering addict realizes deeply that what was received was a gift—one that was nothing, if not pure grace.

7. From Isolation to Community

One member of a twelve-step group reported to me that his recovery meant an end to what he described as a life of "isolation." He described being isolated from himself, others, and God and lived in his own world. Recovery has been a long and at times painful process for many, but one which has gradually led to the awareness that real joy in living comes in and through real communion. Seeking recovery from addictions is a crisis that forces one out of hiding and into the light of truth. What makes this recovery possible is the hope that is born out of the twelve-step community. One person in recovery for several years put it this way: "I'm glad there is a place I can go and share how I feel and not feel judged." Healing comes through connecting with others, albeit a sponsor in the twelve-step program or another member of the group.

Research seems to support this psychospiritual dynamic of isolation to communion with others as key to long-term recovery. Oliver Morgan, in his article "Addiction and Spirituality in Context," cites research by Hennessey-Hein (1995) that studied persons with an average of 19.5 years in recovery. She noted dynamics such as a "gradual perceptual shift" from an isolated self to a self-in-relation, a shift from self-destructive behaviors to life-enhancing ones, and the beginnings of a "new life." The recovering women she interviewed spoke about spirituality as being more "connected" to others and to a presence or source of power that fueled continual growth.

Twelve-step recovery groups state in their promises this crucial idea of leaving isolation and drawing closer to others. As described in the *Big Book* of AA, they offer shared experiences of strength and hope and discover such promises as "a new freedom and a new happiness...no longer denying the past or wishing to shut the door on it, they see how their experiences can benefit others...uselessness and self-pity will slip away and they gain insight into their fellows."

Addiction is a shame-bound disease. It hides and avoids the light of truth. God's action in our lives calls us to face the darkness without fear, to come into the light and experience forgiveness and transformation. At the root of recovery is a courageous journey out of self-centered preoccupation toward genuine care for others. This happens through a beloved community. Recovery involves coming home to the center of one's deepest truth, of reclaiming one's deepest identity in communion with others and with the God of one's understanding.

Ego is a problem for those who struggle with addictions. Ego is the sum of all our identifications, and with substance abuse the attachment is to the substance, the greatest love of all. The problem of the ego is the need for control. The more insecure we may feel, the more compelled to try to control our world. We may become gods unto ourselves. The twelve-step form of spirituality recognizes a psychological and spiritual truth: To be fully human is to live in relationship. The isolated "I" finds hope by recognizing the need for community. This is why the first of the twelve steps states that "we" are powerless, not "I." It is a reminder that the way out of alienation and isolation is in a supportive and accepting community, not through one's own resources alone.

> **"The twelve-step form of spirituality recognizes a psychological and spiritual truth: To be fully human is to live in relationship."**

Conclusion

In sum, psychospiritual recovery from addiction involves a fundamental recognition that at the heart of the addictive process is a lost soul traveling down a path seeking peace and an absence from life's pain, yet ultimately destined for greater alienation from self, others, and God. At the root of the compulsive and addictive pattern is a self that feels incomplete, insecure, and lacking adequate resources to cope with life's many changes, losses, and challenges. The direction of that search is clearly misguided by false idols or attachments that promise quick answers to life's complexities and suffering. Hope lies in recognizing these psychological and spiritual maladies that plague the lost soul.

Those most vulnerable are those whose histories suggest a compulsive pattern. Shame is often at the root, and healing involves a gradual psychospiritual recovery process of acceptance and forgiveness rooted in humility. Defenses like denial and projection make any intervention

challenging, but to confront lovingly is to model the depths of true caring. This form of "tough love" means that ministers and others who seek to offer healing will have to take the risk of rejection and misunderstanding in the interest of truth, justice, and mercy.

The challenge for seminaries, churches, and other pastoral ministers is to remain creatively involved in the ministry to persons and families struggling with addictions of all sorts. This ministry will involve being able to witness, live, and proclaim a counter cultural message of true peace rooted in love, tolerance, forgiveness, and mercy. The church can assist by modeling in their own lives a healthy form of relationally motivated asceticism that offers a spiritual way through the desert of pain and isolation toward our home with others and God.

There are multiple creative ways to minister, from incorporating addictions into homilies, to offering church space for twelve-step groups, to pastoral counseling, to working toward prevention efforts and systemic change. Whatever the way, those preparing for leadership ministry in the church today must be adequately trained to both recognize and begin to heal their own compulsive behaviors, as well as minister compassionately to the many persons and families impacted by addiction. An attitude of openness that sees the addictive journey as a misguided spiritual quest will leave one better equipped to respond in non-judgmental and more effective ways.

Kevin P. McClone, M.Div., Psy.D., is a licensed clinical psychologist, certified alcohol and drug counselor, and certified chaplain who has worked for over twenty years in the health care field. Kevin currently is the director of the Institute for Sexuality Studies located on the campus of Catholic Theological Union where he has provided seminars on psychology and sexuality and tutored religious and lay men and women from around the world. He is also an adjunct faculty member for both Catholic Theological Union and National Luis University in Chicago.

Bibliography

Alcoholics Anonymous. *The Big Book.* 4th ed. New York: A. A. World Service, Inc. This is considered the basic text of Alcoholics Anonymous.

_____. *Twelve Steps and Twelve Traditions.* New York: Harper & Row, 1952.

Carnes, Patrick. *Out of the Shadows: Understanding Sexual Addiction.* Center City, MN: Hazelton, 1992.

Carnes, Patrick. *In the Shadow of the Net: Breaking Free of Compulsive Online Sexual Behavior.* Center City, MN: Hazelton, 2001.

Clinebell, Howard. *Understanding and Counseling Persons with Alcohol, Drug, and Behavioral Addictions.* Rev. ed. Nashville, TN: Abington Press, 1998.

Knapp, Caroline. *Drinking: A Love Story.* New York: The Dial Press, 1996.

Kurtz, Ernest and Katherine Ketchum. *A Spirituality of Imperfection.* New York, NY: Bantam Books, 1992.

May, Gerald, M.D. *Addiction and Grace.* San Francisco, CA: Harper & Row, 1988.

Morgan & Jordan, eds. *Addiction and Spirituality: A Multidisciplinary Approach.* St. Louis, MO: Chalice Press, 1999.

Presnall, Lewis. *The Search for Serenity.* Salt Lake City, UT: Utah Alcoholism Foundation, 1959.

Is the Problem Alcohol or Another Addiction?

Michael Morton, M.A.

This article is reprinted from Seminary Journal, *Volume 9, Winter 2003.*

Throughout the course of human history, alcohol and other drugs have played a significant role in individual and collective behavior. The United States from the time of Western European settlement to the present has been heavily influenced by the consumption of "spirits." As early as 1784, Dr. Benjamin Rush, the father of American Psychiatry and a signer of the Declaration of Independence, described the unhealthy drinking habits of Americans and the high incidence of medical problems and death as a result of alcohol consumption. He diagnosed the problem of habitual drinking as an involuntary condition, a disease caused by "spirituous liquor." He further considered the illness as "physical, psychological, and metaphysical." In *The Varieties of Religious Experience,* William James described alcoholics as frustrated mystics searching to make meaning in their lives. The solution for the alcoholic and addict today is recognized as having a strong spiritual basis.

Catholic initiatives to limit the damage of alcoholism through history are numerous, for example, the temperance movements in England, Ireland, and the United States. Efforts continue in various organizations such as the National Catholic Council on Alcoholism and Related Drug Problems, Inc. The NCCA, originally founded in 1949 as The National Clergy Conference on Alcoholism, was organized in response to the unmet needs of suffering alcoholics. The mission of the NCCA is education about the problem and hope of preventing the spread of alcoholism as well as understanding and treatment for the illness. Catholic clergy and religious have had a strong presence and influence in the development and growth of the most successful and universal fellowship established to help alcoholics, Alcoholics Anonymous.

Today we know that all addictive and compulsive behaviors share certain characteristics, although alcohol remains the drug of choice for the majority of Americans.

In the United States, according to the National Institute on Alcoholism:

- Alcohol is used by more Americans than any other drug, including cigarette tobacco.
- An estimated 10.5 million adults in America exhibit symptoms of alcoholism. An additional 7.2 million abuse alcohol, but do not show signs of dependence. Roughly 1 in 13 adults abuses alcohol or is alcoholic.
- The annual economic cost in 1991 for alcohol abuse and dependence was estimated to be $128 billion. According to researchers (Harwood, 2000), the estimated cost in 1998 was $184.6 billion, including health care expenditures, productivity impacts, motor vehicle crashes, crime, fire destruction, and social welfare administration.

- Alcohol affects almost every organ in the body, and its abuse is associated with a wide variety of diseases, including liver disease, cancer, brain damage, and cardiovascular problems.
- Aside from physical and social problems, there is extensive evidence that prolonged alcohol consumption in some individuals impairs judgment and leads to an array of psychological and emotional disorders. The implications for this point are profound in the professional community as well as tragic to many who suffer from addictive disorders.

> **"'Alcoholism is a chronic, progressive, and a potentially fatal disease. It is characterized by tolerance and physical dependency or pathologic organ changes, or both, all the direct or indirect consequences of the alcohol ingested.'"**

Defining the Problem

In 1972, the National Council on Alcoholism published its seminal article titled "Criteria for the Diagnosis of Alcoholism." The definition of alcoholism prepared by the National Council on Alcoholism and the American Medical Society on Alcoholism followed this in 1976. Emphasizing the progressive nature of the disease, the physical sequelae of alcohol use, and the phenomena of tolerance and withdraw, it stated, "Alcoholism is a chronic, progressive, and a potentially fatal disease. It is characterized by tolerance and physical dependency or pathologic organ changes, or both, all the direct or indirect consequences of the alcohol ingested."

The *Journal of the American Medical Association* published a revised definition of Alcoholism in 1992 based upon the findings of a 23-member multi-disciplinary committee of the National Council on Alcoholism and Drug Dependence and the American Society of Addiction Medicine. This committee attempted to incorporate the vast amount of knowledge learned via research and clinical experience as well as come to an acceptable and useful definition clarifying the characteristics of alcohol abuse and dependency as a disease. It desired a definition that would be scientifically valid, clinically useful, and understandable to the general public. It was aware of the diversity of opinion and problems with clinical judgment in diagnosis and treatment.

The committee agreed to define alcoholism as a primary, chronic disease with genetic, psychosocial, and environmental factors influencing its development and manifestations. The disease is often progressive and fatal. It is characterized by impaired control over drinking, preoccupation with the drug alcohol, use of alcohol in spite of adverse consequences, and distortions in thinking, most notably denial. Each of these symptoms may be continuous or periodic. (JAMA, 1992)

The Three Cs

The three factors most often associated with addiction and dependency are:

Compulsion—a mental obsession or preoccupation to perform a certain act such as taking a drug or drinking.

Loss of Control—the inability to predict or judge appropriate use of alcohol in terms of social context, as well as the quantity consumed and the duration of the drinking or drugging episode.

Continuance—in spite of adverse consequence such as medical, occupational, or legal ramifications. Continuance is a hallmark of addictive behavior that is confounding to everyone, including the addict who has lost control.

Dependency and Abuse

An important aspect of the new criteria for alcohol dependency in the *Diagnostic and Statistical Manual of Mental Disorders (*DSMIV) is that tolerance and physical withdrawal are not necessary criteria to diagnose alcohol dependency. "Neither tolerance nor withdrawal is necessary or sufficient for a diagnosis of Substance Dependency. Some individuals show a pattern of compulsive use without any signs of tolerance or withdraw."

Several important distinctions are to be made between the abuse of alcohol and other drugs. Abuse does not involve the same cravings, compulsions, and physical dependency and tolerance realized by the chronic drinker. Indicators of abuse are:

- Failure to fulfill major work, school, or home responsibilities.
- Drinking in situations that are physically dangerous, such as driving a car.
- Recurring alcohol-related legal problems, such as being arrested for driving under the influence or hurting someone while drunk.
- Continued drinking in spite of ongoing relationship problems that are caused or worsened by the effects of alcohol.

In light of our original question, *"Is Alcohol the Problem?"* the evidence is overwhelming for the high probability of a "yes" in many situations. Although the medical establishment and general public have become much more aware, addiction remains a common problem in a culture of denial. The criteria for abuse and dependency are valuable markers for those responsible for the welfare of another who will most often deny and hide the exact nature of the problem. Addiction continues to be overlooked or minimized in light of many of the crises for which it is the causative factor. This was discovered to be the case in a study at a major teaching hospital where less than six percent of emergency room admissions were screened for addictive disorders! This particular hospital treats patients from some of the most drug-addicted communities in America.

In the professional community there remains some denial and confusion about the nature of addiction as a primary problem. This confusion in collusion with the denial of the addicted person exacerbates the difficult job of diagnosis and intervention. In many cases, the potential for abuse is minimized as a lesser problem than mental or emotional illness and behavioral disorders. In other instances, those in authority are simply "tired out by problem drinkers." They have a

feeling of being defeated by the active drinker or addict and so it seems easier to surrender and allow the situation to continue or deny the nature of the problem.

Some Basic Principles

Sound clinical judgment calls for ruling out problems due to a medical condition and, secondly, problems due to alcohol and other drugs. The associated risk factors of allowing one to continue to drink when there are signs and symptoms of abuse or dependency raise ethical questions, not to mention major risk management issues. One needs to be informed by current research and trends in consumption and abuse among the general population. Factors conducive to addiction such as isolation, stress, trauma, and burnout are common among religious and clergy. The alarming rate of addiction due to prescribed drugs among the elderly also needs to be considered. To not intervene or to believe the problem of addiction among religious and clergy has been resolved is simply to delay the inevitable consequences for inaction.

Possible Reasons for Resisting Identification and Intervention

The classic cause for discretion being the better part of valor in identification and intervention is the simple reluctance to risk being wrong. A list of others may involve the following:

- Being disliked, being attacked
- Becoming involved in a potentially long process
- Opening a bag of worms, discovering other problems
- Losing personnel, being burdened with someone's responsibilities while in treatment
- Fearing the process will result in failure
- Being blamed for mishandling of the case
- Knowing the identified person is not the only one with the problem
- The perceived cost of treatment
- Disgust or disdain for the alcoholic
- Guilt that you are "ruining someone's future"
- Questioning one's own motivation
- Loyalty to the alcoholic/addict
- The "real problem" is something else

In the history of alcohol treatment, it is not the case that those "forced" into treatment do poorly. In fact, alcoholics who experienced the early forms of intervention and inpatient treatment were frequently court-committed. The literature describes the added leverage of such commitment for the person to accept treatment. The chief impediment to recovery for the addictive person is refusal to accept help. This frequently means a difficult and unpleasant task for anyone willing to set up an intervention. Addicts do not give up addiction without a struggle. Usually there is a great deal of anger and prolonged passive resistance designed to wear out the person trying to help.

A continuing factor in the minimization of current addiction is the irrational belief that after many people are treated the remaining people are not addicted—a type of hopeful expectation that the problem is solved! The problem is ever ancient, ever new. There is ample evidence in history that addiction is around for the duration of our existence. The United States correctional system presently involves about six million persons on any given day, according to Department of Justice statistics. Many who work in these systems know the relationship of addiction to the present crisis.

> ## "Treating problems other than alcoholism does not necessarily keep a person from abusing alcohol or other drugs. In fact, primary treatment for addiction is the recommended first step to resolving other problems."

Treating problems other than alcoholism does not necessarily keep a person from abusing alcohol or other drugs. In fact, primary treatment for addiction is the recommended first step to resolving other problems. Responsible treatment for alcoholism addresses other issues when these may interfere with continued sobriety. The

experience of treating other issues as primary may appear to work but usually entails a general progression of all problems when the addict is allowed to continue to drink. Little can be gained from any therapeutic intervention while a person is actively drinking.

Michael Morton, M.A., L.M.F.T., is an educator, trainer, and licensed family therapist with more than 30 years experience in helping individuals, institutions, and families. He enjoys a national reputation presenting and training professionals, organizations, and groups with special needs. He is the director of education and training for Guest House, an addiction treatment center for Catholic clergy and religious in Lake Orion, Michigan.

Bibliography

Alcoholics Anonymous. *Twelve Steps and Twelve Traditions*. New York, 1981.

Fearing, James. *Workplace Intervention: The Bottom Line on Helping Addicted Employees Become Productive Again*. Center City, MN: Hazelden, 2000.

Fichter, Joseph, SJ. *The Rehabilitation of Clergy Alcoholics: Ardent Spirits Subdued*. New York: Human Science Press, 1982.

Furton, J. Edward, and Veronica McCloud Dort, eds. *Addiction and Compulsive Behaviors: Proceedings of the Seventeenth Workshop for Bishops*. Boston, MA: The National Catholic Bioethics Center, 2000.

Johnson, Vernon. *I'll Quit Tomorrow: A Practical Guide to Alcoholism Treatment*. Rev. ed. New York: Harper and Row, 1980.

May, Gerald, M.D. *Addiction & Grace*. New York: Harper and Row, 1988.

Milkman, Harvey, and Stanely Sunderwirth. *Craving for Ecstasy: How Our Passions Become Addictions and What We Can Do About Them*. San Francisco, CA: Josey-Bass, 1987.

Morse, Robert, M.D., and Daniel Flavin, M.D. "The Definition of Alcoholism." *The Journal of the American Medical Association*, August 1992 (vol. 268).

National Clergy Conference on Alcoholism. *Alcoholism: A Source Book for the Priest, an Anthology*. Indianapolis, IN, 1960.

Vaillant, George. *The Natural History of Alcoholism Revisited*. Cambridge, MA: Harvard University Press, 1995.

Weil, Andrew, M.D., and Winifred Rosen. *From Chocolate To Morphine: Everything You Wanted to know About Mind-Altering Drugs*. Boston, MA: Houghton Mifflin, 1993.

White, William. *Slaying the Dragon: The History of Addiction Treatment and Recovery in America*. Bloomington, IL: Chestnut Health Systems, 1998.

In the Shadows of the Net: Understanding Cybersex in the Seminary

David Delmonico, Ph.D., and Elizabeth Griffin, M.A.

This article is reprinted from Seminary Journal, *Volume 9, Winter 2003.*

Case Example

Don could hardly believe what he was saying to his spiritual director. The descriptions of what he was doing on the Internet seemed as though he was describing someone else. He wondered how things had gotten so out of control. In the past, he had struggled with pornographic magazines, but nothing compared to how he was struggling with cybersex on the Internet. Don's social life was minimal. His grades were suffering. He knew he couldn't continue to lead two lives. In one life he was the model citizen and a good student. In the other, he was lost in an electronic world of lust for nearly four hours every day. He watched his pornography use turn from somewhat manageable to out of control. As he disclosed his problem to his spiritual director, he realized how much worse things could get if he didn't confront the problem.

Introduction

Like so many others, Don underestimated the impact the Internet could have on his sexuality and his life in general. Just a Web site here, a sex chat there, a pornographic email, newsgroup posting, or participation in file sharing—it all seemed so innocent and innocuous. Then, one day, commitments are being sacrificed, loneliness and isolation are a daily reality, and controlling

> **"The relationships formed are pseudo-relationships requiring little emotional investment and can be terminated with the click of a mouse."**

the behavior is a thing of the past. Obsessed with finding that one image, that one conversation, or that one person who holds the key to happiness and fulfillment, life spirals out of control. Hours pass as you seek the ultimate high—perfect sex on the Internet. The pursuit is illusive, however, since the Internet feeds fantasy, not reality. The relationships formed are pseudo-relationships requiring little emotional investment and can be terminated with the click of a mouse.

Fortunately, in Don's situation, he talked to someone. He broke the secrecy and isolation and sought help because he recognized how quickly the electronic world consumed him. Unfortunately, there are millions of others who do not recognize the danger until it is too late. Their lives and the lives of those around them are shattered.

This article introduces the basic concepts of cybersex and discusses the implications of cybersex in seminary formation. Although cybersex compulsivity is a relatively new and unexplored field, what is known may be helpful in identifying, preventing, and intervening with seminary students such as Don, who feel they are out of control with cybersex behavior.

Statistics

Although research regarding Internet behavior is unwieldy, best estimates suggest there are nearly 250 million users who sign on regularly to the Internet (Nielsen Netratings, September, 2003). There are approximately 100,000 Web sites dedicated to child pornography, with millions of visitors paying billions of dollars to access their drug of choice—cybersex (Grove & Zerega, 2002). No group of individuals is unaffected by online sexuality, including the Christian community. For pastors, 51% reported that cyberporn was a temptation, while 37% reported it being a current struggle (Gardner, 2001). One of every seven calls to the "Pastoral Care Hotline" is related to Internet pornography (Focus on the Family, 2003). Clergy reporting problems with cybersex tended to be younger and report spending about 12 hours a week online in sexual pursuits (Gardner, 2001).

The Internet is a way of life for younger generations. Just as television is an integral part of our society, microcomputers and high-speed Internet connections have moved into homes, schools, and public places, allowing access to millions of pages of information to millions of individuals.

The following sections describe the how, who, and why of cybersex.

Accessing Cybersex

There are many ways to access cybersex on the Internet. Leaders and helping professionals who have a basic understanding of the multiple methods of access will be more helpful to those struggling with Internet sexuality. This basic knowledge allows faculty advisors, spiritual directors, and others to ask pertinent questions using the language of the Internet. Delmonico and Griffin (in press) presented the various methods for accessing cybersex on the Internet.

World Wide Web. The most common form of access to the Internet is via the World Wide

> **"Leaders and helping professionals who have a basic understanding of the multiple methods of access will be more helpful to those struggling with Internet sexuality."**

Web. Internet browsers (e.g., Netscape, Internet Explorer, Opera, etc.) allow the user to view Web pages that may contain pornographic text, sounds, or images. Many people equate the World Wide Web with the Internet, but in fact, it is only one method of accessing information on the Internet.

Newsgroups. This area serves as a bulletin board where individuals can post and read text or multimedia messages, such as pictures, sounds, and video.

Email. Email can be used for direct communication with other individuals or groups of individuals. In the case of cybersex, the message may be a sexual conversation. story, picture, sound, or video. Often individuals meet in other areas of the Internet and then begin communicating via email.

Chat Rooms. Both sexualized conversation and multimedia can be exchanged in chat rooms. Casual users are familiar with Web-based chatting such as Yahoo Chat or America Online (AOL) Chat. Most Web-based chat areas have sections dedicated to sexual chats. However, the largest chat-based system is the Internet Relay Chat (IRC), an area largely unfamiliar to most casual users. In addition to text-based chatting, IRC contains a number of chat rooms specifically dedicated to the exchange of pornography through "file servers."

Videoconferencing / Voice Chatting. The use of these areas is rapidly increasing. As technology improves and connection speeds increase, the use of the Internet for "live" cybersex sessions will become commonplace. Videoconferencing, combined with voice chat, represents a high tech version of a peep show and obscene phone call mixed into one.

Peer to Peer File Sharing. Software packages such as Napster® and Kazaa® have made file sharing a popular hobby. Casual users of this software know its use for exchanging music files, but any file can be "shared" on the network. Many of the files on these networks are pornographic in nature. These pornographic files are numerous, easily found, and can contain illegal child pornography. In fact, one study reported that 42% of all Kazaa requests were for either adult or child pornography (Brown, 2003).

Online Gaming. Online destinations such as MOOs and MUDs encourage participants to take on various characters and play out their roles in a game-like setting. Some of these game areas are sexually charged and offer places for participants to engage in sexual conversations. Some individuals become compulsive with the fantasy, role-playing aspect of these games, whether sexual or not.

How an individual accesses cybersex is one aspect of assessing the problematic use of the Internet. However, not all cybersex users are equal. The next section will discuss the various categories of cybersex users.

> **"Since many seminary students are in late adolescence/early adulthood, they are often at a critical juncture in their sexual development."**

Cybersex User Categories

Carnes, Delmonico, & Griffin (2001) presented the cybersex user categories (Figure 1). The model is not empirically created but, rather, theoretically based on a variety of research surveys and clinical evidence. Several other models of conceptualizing the types of online users exist, most of which address similar categories of users even though they may use different words to describe the groups.

In one of the largest studies of Online Sexual Activity (OSA), Cooper, Delmonico, & Burg (2000)

Figure I

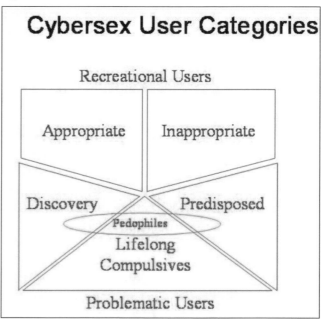

found that the majority (80%) reported little or no consequences in their lives and did not report any significant life area in jeopardy due to cybersex use. While one could argue that these individuals may be denying or minimizing the impact of cybersex, it should be stated that not everyone who engages in OSA does so at a pathological or problematic level.

Lisa was married for eight years. She and her husband Jason had two children, and they were happy. However, they felt that the romance and intimacy had left their relationship. One night, while logged on to the Internet, Lisa suggested she and her husband search for ways to enhance their sexual relationship. Together they chatted with other couples about ways to improve their sex life. They shopped for new sexual toys that might re-ignite their sexual spark. They even viewed some soft-core pornography sites to get some ideas for sexual positions and behaviors that might be appealing to each of them. They approached their sexual life with new understanding and enthusiasm.

Although there may have been other ways for Lisa and Jason to explore their sexual relationship, little apparent harm came from exploring via the Internet in a safe, private environment. Many individuals use the Internet for sexual information and exploration. In fact, 70%-75% of adolescents reported using the Internet to get sexual information (Kaiser Family

Foundation, 2001). Albeit preferable for teenagers to talk to parents or other trusted adults, research demonstrates this seldom happens. For adolescents who know where to find accurate information, the Internet becomes an avenue for accessing reliable sexual information rather than relying on inaccurate peer anecdotes.

Since many seminary students are in late adolescence/early adulthood, they are often at a critical juncture in their sexual development. At this stage of development there are numerous questions about their body, spirituality, and sexual relationships. For some, the Internet may be a healthy way to explore sexuality in a safe environment; for others, it may present a dangerous area of exploration. While it is not possible to predict who will become a problematic user of cybersex, the following user categories help identify the predisposed and lifelong sexual compulsives who would certainly be at higher risk than other categories.

Discovery Group. The discovery group includes those who have never had any problems with sexual fantasy or behavior until they discovered sex on the Internet. Sex on the Internet fostered the development of compulsive behavior they may not have otherwise experienced. Although this group is rare, it does exist, and little can be done to predict problematic cybersex for the "Discovery User."

Predisposed Group. The predisposed group is composed of individuals who have had some history of problematic sexual thoughts or fantasies, but have the coping mechanisms in place to keep their sexual urges and behaviors under control. The Internet fosters the development of an already existing, out-of-control sexual fantasy or urge that may not have developed into actual problematic behavior without the Internet. The case of Don (above) is a good example of a predisposed user. He admitted he had a history of fantasy urges or behaviors involving pornography.

Lifelong Sexually Compulsive Group. The lifelong sexually compulsive group is composed of those who have dealt with sexually compulsive behavior throughout their life, and the Internet simply becomes one additional way of acting out their inappropriate sexual behaviors.

This group often has well-established patterns of problematic sexual urges, fantasies, and behaviors and a history of ritualized sexually problematic behaviors. Some individuals in this group may see cybersex as a "safer" way of acting out their problematic sexual behaviors since it may reduce their direct contact with others. This may happen for a short period of time, but in many cases individuals in this group will eventually return to sexually problematic behaviors offline.

> **"70%-80% of individuals reported keeping the amount of time they spend online secret from others in their lives."**

Why Individuals Become Compulsive

Understanding who uses cybersex is only one part of the equation. The following section discusses some possibilities for why individuals become compulsive with their Internet sexuality. Delmonico, Griffin, and Moriarty (2001) proposed the "CyberHex of the Internet" (Figure 2) to explain the powerful attraction of the Internet.

Integral. Integral suggests the Internet is nearly impossible to avoid. Even if a cybersex user decided never to use the Internet again, the integral nature of the Internet would make that boundary nearly impossible. The reality is that most individuals have jobs that require Internet access. In addition, public availability, the use of email, and other activities like shopping and research make the Internet a way of life that is integrated into our daily routines.

Imposing. The amount of general information found on the Internet is staggering. This is true of sexual material as well. The Internet provides an endless supply of sexual material 7 days a week, 365 days a year. The amount of information and the imposing nature of marketing sexual information on the Internet contribute to being drawn into the world of cybersex.

Inexpensive. For a relatively small fee, $20 to $40 per month, one can access an intoxicating

Figure 2—CyberHex of the Internet

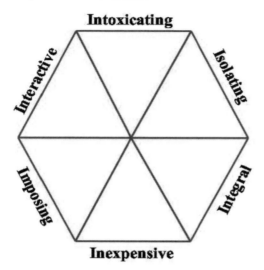

amount of sexual material on the Internet. In the offline world such excursions can prove to be extremely expensive and cost prohibitive to many. The Internet overrides the cost prohibition.

Isolating. Cybersex is an isolating activity. Even though interpersonal connections may be made during the course of cybersex, these relationships do not require the same level of social skills, interaction, or basic intimacy that offline behaviors require. The Internet becomes a world into itself, where it is easy to lose track of time, consequences, and real life relationships. The isolation of cybersex often provides an escape from the real world, and while everyone takes short escapes, cybersex often becomes the "drug of choice" to anesthetize negative feelings associated with real life relationships.

Interactive. While isolating in nature, the Internet also hooks individuals into forming pseudo-relationships. These pseudo-relationships often approximate reality without running the risks of real relationships: emotional and physical vulnerability and intimacy. This close approximation to reality can be fuel for the fantasy life of those who experience problems with their cybersex behaviors.

Intoxicating. This is the phenomenon that occurs when you add together the first five elements of the Cyberhex. This combination makes for an incredibly intoxicating element that is often difficult for many to resist. The intoxication of the Internet is multiplied when cybersex is involved, since behaviors are reinforced with one of the most powerful rewards, sex.

> **"'Do you use online chat rooms as a way to relieve feelings of isolation and loneliness?'"**

Characteristics of Vulnerable Clergy

Jasper felt he was called to serve God as a priest at age 14, only two years after having been sexually abused by an older male neighbor. Even though he was now only 21 years old, he had always dreamed of having a parish of his own one day so that he could lead others towards God. Because he knew he would take a vow of celibacy, he never experimented with romantic relationships and had set a boundary with himself not to explore his own sexuality. After several years in seminary, Jasper struggled with sexual fantasies and masturbation, but was always able to manage them.

One day, while researching for a paper in school, he found an extremely explicit pornography site on the Internet. The floodgates opened and within weeks he found himself spending several hours each day searching for online pornography. Jasper reassured himself that he was just curious and that he would soon be back to "normal." After several months of compulsive masturbation and Internet sex, his behavior escalated into urges to find a prostitute and act out sexually. No one knew that Jasper was in danger. He had managed to keep his double life a secret.

Cooper, Delmonico, and Burg (2000) reported that nearly 70%-80% of individuals reported keeping the amount of time they spend online secret from others in their lives. If this is true for the lay population, think of how much more protected the secrets of a seminary student must be. Whether they have taken a vow of celibacy or not, sexual issues are often difficult to discuss, especially for individuals who are in a profession that is often regarded as holy and asexual.

Laaser (1991) and Davies (2003) highlighted certain characteristics of clergy that make them vulnerable to sexually addictive behaviors. These characteristics also may apply to sexually acting out on the Internet. Laaser's and Davies' characteristics are combined and listed below:

- Hope that their ordination would reduce the shame they feel in their lives.

- Are codependents who seek approval from others and get their needs met by gaining widespread approval by pleasing parishioners.

- Are in significant denial regarding their sexual issues. The consequences for clergy are more profound when it comes to sexual indiscretions.

- Often have well-entrenched rigid judgmental thinking that is buttressed by their theology.

- Often have a great deal of unexpressed anger.

- See themselves as shameful, bad, or unworthy.

- Use sex to take care of their emotional needs.

- Often have predisposing factors that lead to the development of these characteristics. Some of these predisposing factors are:

    ✦ Survivors of childhood sexual, physical, or emotional abuse/abandonment.

    ✦ Highly rigid and disengaged families.

    ✦ Rigid spiritual formation from family or others in authority (spiritual abuse).

Consider the above case of Jasper. Jasper's own sexual abuse as an adolescent may have delayed his sexual and emotional development. While God certainly could have called Jasper to ministry, Jasper may have sought ordination in response to the shame and guilt he felt around his sexuality. Jasper's lack of healthy exploration of his sexuality also may have contributed to delayed development. When Jasper discovered Internet pornography, he felt unable to control his urge to explore. In an analogous way, Jasper went from being sexually anorexic (Carnes, 1997) to sexually bulimic. Jasper began to increase the risk involved with his sexual behavior, and began fighting the internal struggle to move online behavior to offline sexual encounters with

prostitutes. Without intervention, Jasper is extremely vulnerable to continued sexual escalation both online and offline.

It is important to note there is no magic formula to determine which clergy are at risk and which are not. There are many clergy who have been abused in childhood and come from disengaged families who are not vulnerable to sexual acting out. However, the predispositions combined with the close interpersonal contacts, isolation (retreats, prayer, private meetings with parishioners, etc.) can certainly make clergy more vulnerable.

> **"Although cybersex is an unpleasant and often embarrassing issue to address, seminaries that address it appropriately will reap the benefits of sexually healthy pastors who can pass their knowledge and awareness on to those they serve."**

What Seminaries Should Know and Do

First and foremost, seminaries should be familiar with the warning signs of cybersex behaviors. The use of the Internet Sex Screening Test (ISST, Delmonico, 1997) may be useful for students who are vulnerable to cybersex behaviors. More important, however, is the willingness to discuss sexual issues and ask questions about a student's computer/Internet use. Questions such as "Do you intentionally visit sexual sites on the Internet?" or "Do you use online chat rooms as a way to relieve feelings of isolation and loneliness?" may be a good starting point with those suspected of having difficulty with their Internet behavior.

Several things often stifle this type of questioning. First, lack of awareness that there may be a problem with the Internet and, second, lack of a desire to discuss sexual issues as part of spiritual formation. In addition, occasionally the spiritual director may have a similar problem with compulsive use of the Internet and not want to draw attention to himself by asking these types of questions or engaging in self disclosure. Whatever the reason, it is important for seminaries to educate themselves about how cybersex can significantly interfere with spiritual formation and prepare a curriculum or intervention strategy to deal directly with this issue.

Ways to Address and Prevent Internet Problems

Rafferty (2003) suggested several ways to address broader Internet problems with clergy and in the seminary. These suggestions can be adapted easily to include cybersex and cyberpornography.

First, Rafferty (2003) suggested that seminary admission offices not be timid about asking direct questions regarding the applicants' use of the Internet. Specifically, questions regarding cybersex could also be included in such an interview. Addressing the issue in the admissions process lets the applicant know the seminary is aware of such problems and may make it easier for the student to come forward if faced with such problems now or in the future.

Second, Rafferty (2003) noted that seminaries should include the moral and ethical use of the Internet and computer. He wrote, "Students need an intellectual basis from which to evaluate the diverse potential of the Internet, both positive and negative" (p. 30).

Third, seminary students should be educated as to the potential consequences of the use of the Internet. In particular, cybersex users could benefit from such consequence awareness and victim empathy education. Many times users of cybersex see their behavior as a victimless act, when in fact there are often many victims involved.

Fourth, seminary leaders should be educated and aware of various cybersex issues, including the warning signs, potential interventions, and available community resources for those struggling with cybersex. This is particularly important since college students are often more vulnerable to cybersex for several reasons. For example, students have easy access at the university, are required to research more information online and spend more time online, use it to contact

family and friends, and often are at a critical stage in their sexual development. Many college-age students use the Internet to explore sexuality and may begin to substitute the online world for the real world, often with a negative impact on their social skill development.

Finally, Rafferty (2003) suggested that seminaries create acceptable use policies (AUP) that specifically designate proper and improper use of the Internet. These policies should address sexual use of the Internet and outline consequences of any infraction of the AUP. The information technology department at the seminary should conduct periodic checks to ensure that faculty, staff, and students are adhering to the policies set forth in the AUP.

Conclusions

Sexually compulsive use of the Internet is a concern for individuals of any age, gender, or profession. The cleric profession is no exception. The first step is admitting that cybersex behaviors can be a problem for pastors and students in seminaries. Most spiritual sectors have difficulty dealing directly with sexual issues, so increasing awareness and developing a healthy willingness to address the issue of cybersex may be the biggest hurdle to helping those who struggle.

Using the above-mentioned cybersex user categories, the Cyberhex, the Internet Screening Test, and suggestions adapted from Rafferty (2003) will prove to be the best course of action for seminaries concerned about sexual use of the Internet by their students.

Although cybersex is an unpleasant and often embarrassing issue, seminaries that address it appropriately will reap the benefits of sexually healthy pastors who can pass their knowledge and awareness on to those they serve.

David Delmonico, Ph.D., is an assistant professor in the Department of Counseling, Psychology, and Special Education at Duquesne University in Pittsburgh, Pennsylvania. Dr. Delmonico is an internationally recognized researcher, author, and speaker in the area of online sexual behaviors. He is the co-author of *In the Shadows of the Net* and *Cybersex Unhooked*, director of the Online Behavior Research and Education Center, and editor-in-chief of the *Sexual Addiction & Compulsivity Journal*.

Elizabeth Griffin, M.A., L.M.F.T., is a licensed Marriage and Family Therapist with more than seventeen years experience treating individuals with sexual issues. Ms. Griffin lectures and consults nationally on the assessment and treatment of those with sexually compulsive behaviors and sexual offending behaviors, as well as issues related to cybersex. She has co-authored a book with Dr. Patrick Carnes and Dr. David Delmonico titled *In the Shadows of the Net: Breaking Free of Compulsive Online Sexual Behavior*, as well as a workbook titled *Cybersex Unhooked*.

References

Brown, S. (2003). Executive summary: Peer-to-peer study results. *Palisades Systems, Inc.* (Last retrieved on November 10, 2003 from http://www.palisadesys.com/news&events/p2pstudy.pdf.)

Carnes, P. J. (1997). *Sexual Anorexia: Overcoming sexual self hatred.* Center City, MN: Hazelden.

Carnes, P. J., Delmonico, D. L., & Griffin, E. J. (2001). *In the shadows of the net: Breaking free of compulsive online sexual behavior.* Center City, MN: Hazelden Publishing.

Cooper, A., Delmonico, D. & Burg, R. (2000). Cybersex users, abusers, and compulsives: New findings and implications. *Sexual Addiction and Compulsivity: Journal of Treatment and Prevention, 7*(1-2), 5-30.

Davies, M. (2003). Clergy sexual addiction: A systemic preventative model. *Sexual Addiction & Compulsivity: The Journal of Treatment and Prevention, 10*(2-3), 99-109.

Delmonico, D. L. (1997). *The Internet Sex Screening Test.* (Last retrieved on November 9, 2003 from http://www.sexhelp.com.)

Delmonico, D. L., & Griffin, E. J. (in press). Cybersex. *Human Computer Interaction Encyclopedia.* Berkshire Press.

Delmonico, D. L., Griffin, E. J., & Moriarity, J. (2001). *Cybersex unhooked: A workbook for breaking free of compulsive online sexual behavior.* Wickenburg, AZ: Gentle Path Press.

Focus on the Family. (2003). Where can I get help for my growing problem with Internet pornography? Author. (Last retrieved on November 9, 2003 from http://www.family.org/pastor/faq.)

Gardner, C. J. (2001, March 5). Tangled in the worst of the Web. *Christianity Today Magazine.* (Last retrieved on November 9, 2003 from http://www.christianitytoday.com/ct/2001/004.)

Grove, R., & Zerega, B. (2002, January 18). The Lolita problem. *Red Herring Magazine.* (Last retrieved November 9, 2003 from http://www.redherring.com.)

Hall, A., & Parsons, J. (2001). Internet addiction: College student case study using best practices in cognitive behavior therapy. *Journal of Mental Health Counseling, 23*(4), 312-327.

Kaiser Family Foundation. (2001). Generation Rx.com: How young people use the Internet for health information. Author. (Last retrieved on November 10, 2003 from http://www.kff.org/content/2001/20011211a.)

Laaser, M. (1991). Recovering sexually addicted clergy: An introduction. *Pastoral Psychology, 39*(4), 257-258.

Nielsen Netratings. (2003, September). Global Internet index: Average usage. Author. (Last retrieved on November 10, 2003 from http://www.netratings.com.)

Rafferty, J. A. (2002). Internet addiction and seminary formation. *Seminary Journal, 8*(1), 24-33.

A Case for Teaching Sexual Addiction Assessment to Seminarians: Preparation as Confessors and Spiritual Directors

Reverend Richard Chiola, Ph.D.

This article is reprinted from Seminary Journal, *Volume 9, Winter 2003.*

At a communal celebration of reconciliation, a man in his early 40s confesses that he has been viewing porn on the Internet. The minister asks, "How long has this been happening?" The penitent responds, "Since I was 15, I used to look at magazines when I was a kid. For the last several years, I've been looking at the Internet." The minister now has two indicators that the man is caught in a sexual addiction. The first is that the Internet is addictive in itself, and porn on the Internet, especially, leads to compulsively seeking the next high, usually attained by seeking more prurient images. The second indicator is that the habit is long-lived.

So, the priest asks, "Why have you brought this to confession today?" The response is heartbreaking. The man answers, "I'm so ashamed. I was watching the Internet and masturbating. It was about 2 a.m. and my five-year-old daughter came into the room asking for a drink of water. I realized I have to control this problem and I don't know how." Now there is little doubt that the man is addicted to sex. He has commingled two compulsions, pornography and masturbation. He is awake at 2 a.m. seeking his next high. He is continuing to seek the high in the dangerous situation of being found out by his wife and children, and he continues anyway. Typically, his attempts at control have repeatedly failed.

Such simple assessment is possible for most confessors and spiritual directors. Why they need to do it is the point of this article. Sexual addiction is one of the greatest hazards to physical and psychological health within the American population. Sexual addiction is a brain disease, rooted in personal sin, which cries out for forgiveness. In the Rite of Reconciliation, priests regularly hear the confession of sexual sins that may be symptomatic of sexual addiction, and many also deal with these sexual issues in spiritual direction. Patrick Carnes has lead research in sexual addiction for twenty years. He says of those who have successfully recovered from sexual addiction, "What their spiritual life consisted of was as important as practicing it on a regular, even daily, basis. Those whose spiritual lives flourished were also usually active participants in a spiritual community."[1] Priests, as leaders of spiritual communities and ministers of

> "The addictive process is such that the user will be drawn to ever more prurient images in order to achieve the desired high, just as an alcoholic must drink more and more to achieve intoxication."

reconciliation, need to know how to help in this recovery.

The first step is to become familiar with the problem of sexual addiction.[2] Consider the contribution of the Internet to the current growth of compulsive sexual behaviors among the very young and among adults in the workplace. The net is addictive in itself and, beyond that, makes available every variety and dimension of sexual pornography. The addictive process is such that the user will be drawn to ever more prurient images in order to achieve the desired high, just as an alcoholic must drink more and more to achieve intoxication. However, sexual addiction also manifests in other contexts.

Carnes describes the pattern of sexual compulsivity as a cycle of preoccupation with sexual thoughts and fantasies which leads to ritualized behaviors.[3] The ritual may appear innocent enough at first, like going to buy cigarettes. The nicotine, though, is part of the numbing that will end several ritual steps later in anonymous sex. The ritual may begin by checking email at work, but the next step is the compulsive behavior triggered by finding none. The person begins to feel isolated and hits on a site that offers opportunities to chat, and then is meeting to have sex during a lunch break. The arousal accompanying the compulsive hit on the Web site numbs the feeling of isolation and leads to the bigger numbing high of sex. The relief, however, is temporary. After the sexual hookup, the isolation returns with a vengeance and sets in motion feelings of shame and despair while simultaneously deepening the preoccupation with sex or its avoidance. The cycle begins anew.

Carnes offers ten diagnostic criteria for assessing sexual addiction. In summary, they form a long-term pattern of sexual behaviors that create problems in the person's life, but which the person feels unable to control despite serious efforts to do so. Instead of control, the person experiences an increase in the intensity and frequency of the behaviors in order to achieve the desired effect. Preoccupation with sexual thoughts and behaviors interferes with normal functioning, but attempts to suppress this preoccupation and its compulsive acting out bring on "distress, anxiety, restlessness, and irritability."[4]

This pattern is manifest in eleven types of sexual acting out.[5] The more sensational types are sex with children and sex with the exchange of pain. Some types particularly occur in the workplace. They include seductive role-playing; fantasy about co-workers; intrusive sexual advances, gestures, and touch; as well as abusive or inappropriate exercise of power. Some types of sexual addictions occur in the neighborhood and the home. These include exhibitionism, voyeurism, anonymous sex, paying for sex, and trading sex (especially associated with drugs, but also with obtaining position of prestige within groups of young people). Not too surprisingly, the compulsive avoidance of sex is also a manifestation of sexual addiction.

Priests hear the pattern and types of sexual addiction in the sacrament of reconciliation and in spiritual direction. For example, Mark Laaser, director of the Institute for Healthy Sexuality of the American Association of Christian Counselors, recounts the story of Phil, who struggled as a seminarian with both compulsive masturbation and the fear of being a homosexual. Seeking a means of control he brought the problem to his spiritual director. According to Laaser, the spiritual director told Phil, "he should say the rosary five times and the temptation would go away."[6] Though the spiritual director's reported advice may stretch credulity, it is less difficult to believe that it did not help. He did not recognize Phil's particular symptom.

Laaser presents Phil's case as an example of the kind of rigidity that is a symptom of sexual

> **"May recommends that spiritual directors form colleague relationships with healthcare professionals to assure the best care of their clients through appropriate referral for therapy."**

addiction. In fact, Phil, like every addict, would have liked nothing better than to have found the "right" formula to handle his compulsivity. This is another manifestation of the disease, the attempt to rigidly control the symptoms and seek the "right" way to suppress the compulsivity. Phil eventually was ordained and served in a parish. He continued to become even more rigid, especially in his public condemnation of homosexuality. If his spiritual director had known how to deal with the addict's frantic search for control, Phil might have received better care and been better prepared for ministry in Catholic parishes, where one may assume there will be homosexual members, whether closeted or not. Still, the commingling of sexual compulsivity with other compulsions (such as drugs or alcohol) and the complex variety of manifestations (controlling/abusive behaviors of spouse and children, cyclic affairs, indiscriminate homosexual acting out, or even total sexual avoidance/anorexia) makes the underlying addiction particularly difficult to assess.

In spiritual direction, as in psychological counseling, one can explore the feelings, difficulties, strengths, and successes of the person being companioned. The focus in each session is different. Gerald May, a psychiatrist who worked for decades with Sahlem Institute, defines spiritual direction as attention to one's relationship with God and mental healthcare as attention to one's worldview. Both kinds of attending are necessary for treatment of sexual addiction and compulsivity. May recommends that spiritual directors form colleague relationships with healthcare professionals to assure the best care of their clients through appropriate referral for therapy.[7] Still, a

relationship to a higher power is fundamental to handing over control, an essential step in recovery. To relinquish control is particularly essential to the sacrament of reconciliation, but there the time to explore the person's story is limited.

In the Rite of Reconciliation, there is limited time to probe the inner workings of the penitent's story, and even if he had time, the confessor may not think he should ask probing questions. Confessions, although individually private, are usually heard at public communal liturgies or at publicly stated times in places where several persons gather. Penitents often are aware of others waiting to talk to the same priest-confessor. Thus, there is a sense that one should further truncate the list of sins so as not to attract attention to oneself. The brevity of the time with the priest in the rite makes assessment of symptoms more difficult, as does the concern of the confessor not to appear to be grilling the penitent, create fears of sins beyond those confessed, or inflict shame. Yet, it is shame, the addict's self-judgment, which needs to be addressed if the penitent is to experience forgiveness.

Kurt Stasiak, OSB, offers some particularly helpful advice.[8] He lays out several principles for listening to the penitent, particularly the reason the penitent has come to confess. There is a specific reason this person is seeking the freedom of the children of God. What is it? This confession is a unique occasion, a moment that should be attended. Why this moment, this occasion for the confession? Attend not just to the list of sins, but also to the particular struggle revealed in this confession of sins. Most important, let the penitent help you guide the way to the forgiveness being sought. Attend to the reason for the sins confessed, and the confession will reveal much more to you as confessor than the individual sins presented.

But once the questions are asked and there is indication that the penitent may have a sexual addiction, what next? The obvious answer is to refer for counseling so that the person can work through the twelve steps of recovery. Some will be ready for counseling, but not all. Furthermore, referral presumes that well-trained sexual addiction therapists are available. Then there is the question of compliance. Is this a penance, pastoral advice, or just a suggestion? But all of these questions, important as they are, do not address the relationship of sexual addiction to sacramental forgiveness.

The way to forgiveness is surrender, the way of the Paschal Mystery. This path to God is found, as Aquinas always insisted, in the facts of the situation itself. In this case the facts are the symptoms of addiction. The well-prepared confessor recognizes that a gentle assessment can lead the penitent to recognize the pattern of addiction and from there to admit his pathological shame.

It is clear from the research that the foundation of sexual addiction is a judgment which the addict renders against himself. That judgment, given a voice, has four features. The first is that sex is the person's most important need. The reason is the other three: "If others knew who I really am, they would never be able to accept or love me." "I am flawed, an unworthy person." And "My needs will never be met by others, if I simply were to rely on them."[9] This judgment is called shame. Shame is the foundation underlying sex as the drug of choice. It is the opposite of surrender.

Karl Rahner would call the addict's shame a "constitutive sign" of the true sin or guilt.[10] In other words, shame is only evidence of the real guilt the person bears. The shame constitutes an unbearable burden. But it is a double-cross blocking the way to forgiveness and spawning numbing behaviors rather than surrender. In the sacrament of reconciliation, the minister offers the forgiveness of God, the remedy for the true guilt which the addict glimpses in the mirror shame. How can the minister lead the addict through this looking glass to forgiveness of his sin?

The Rite of Reconciliation offers re-immersion into the Paschal Mystery: surrender and accepting the forgiveness of God as the source of one's life. The Christian's response contains the first three steps in the twelve to recovery. For the penitent to enter again into this mystery, first given in baptism, he must confess he cannot control his sexual behavior. His life is out of his control. He cannot deal with the shame. Instead, he numbs it by sexually acting out or runs from it by sexual avoidance/anorexia. He must recognize this pattern if he is to accept forgiveness. Forgiveness presumes a lack of self-control. Forgiveness is God meeting the penitent in the saving grace of Christ and supporting him in developing sobriety. Divine forgiveness is prior to our ability to integrate it into our lives.

If a priest is to help a sex addict accept the potency of divine grace, he must first understand the addiction to sex and how to assess its symptoms. Perhaps it is time to develop a handbook on sexual addiction assessment for seminarians, confessors, and spiritual directors. For instance, how might such a handbook help a formator work with a seminarian like Phil, whose story was mentioned earlier?

"Even if Phil is a sex addict, is an addiction *per se* a disqualifier for ordination?"

We were told that as a seminarian Phil experienced compulsive masturbation and feared that he was homosexual in his orientation. After ordination, he became increasingly strident in his denunciation of homosexuals. Phil is an example, used in addiction literature, of a man seeking control over his compulsivity, a compulsive acting out apparently rooted in fear of his own sexuality. What should the formator do?

In the present situation of continuing fear over more sex scandals and accompanying homophobia, it is understandable that some formators might want to just "weed out" seminarians like Phil. The question is difficult, but it is deeply theological as well. To what extent is the *communio* in the church to be reflected in the care given a man who desires to offer himself for service as a priest but whose compulsions may in fact be an addiction? Even if Phil is a sex addict, is an addiction *per se* a disqualifier for ordination? For an answer, we begin with the sexual addiction literature.

Since 1983, a good deal of the literature on sex addiction has been dedicated to the debate over what to call the compulsive thoughts and acting out that was first labeled "addiction" by

Patrick Carnes in *Out of the Shadows*.[11] Eli Coleman, Jim Orford, and others have been very clear that on the one hand compulsive thoughts and behaviors are part of normal human sexuality and on the other that not all abnormal obsessive compulsive behavior can be rightly called an addiction.[12] Despite our moral stance that masturbation and homosexuality are a disordering of the purpose of human sexuality, any person may and most will have some obsessive thoughts or behaviors around these two issues. For instance, masturbation is not always abnormal or maladaptive behavior; it is within the range of the psychologically normal. It is not necessarily in itself an unmanageable behavior; nonetheless, it has its obsessive tendency. Masturbation can also be an unmanageable addiction with life threatening possibility, especially when accompanied by the use of combinations of drugs like ecstasy and Viagra.

Concern over one's sexual orientation is also a normal aspect of psychosexual development. Joe Kort is particularly clear that in his work with homosexual men the developmental task of sorting out the difference between being attracted to men and being gay is a complex issue that takes a good deal of time and effort for a man to negotiate.[13] Homosexuals can and do live in celibate chastity. A formator would need to do some more discernment with Phil and probably get some expert assistance in order to help him understand exactly what he is dealing with as a man and how he can develop his own life as a celibate.

If Phil is an addict he will need a safe environment to tell his story. Any psychological or spiritual treatment has as its objective the extinguishing of the addict's obsession, but that can be accomplished only by dealing with the addict's belief system, his sense of personal shame in which his compulsive behaviors are rooted. "The purpose of treatment must not be to push the addict into de-escalation, but rather to bring about a *profound shift of beliefs and behaviors* in which the obsession loses its power."[14] For this purpose, developing rapport with the addict is essential.[15] There must be established a safe container in which the addict experiences "psychological safety."[16] The reason is simple. The

> ## "The study functions to warn clinicians and non-clinicians that the level of religious practice of the assessor, as well as the gender, may influence the assessment."

addict's disclosure of his addiction will occur in a convoluted process that moves back and forth in a series of stages that Carnes describes as an initial disclosure, followed by admission of details, then a retraction or minimizing of details, which may lead to further disclosure, further details, or another retraction phase. However, the important first steps to recovery are not the revelation of the details of the addict's behaviors. This kind of revelation will occur only if an initial spiritual change that addresses the addict's belief system had been established. What the addict must do first is accomplish the first three steps in the twelve steps to recovery of a balanced life that are modeled on those developed by Alcoholics Anonymous, the first of many successful non-clinical and spiritually based peer treatment organizations.

It is precisely in the *communio* of the church and through spiritual formation in seminaries that we can offer a man like Phil a safe place to turn his life with all its unmanageability over to God who alone has the power to save us, even from ourselves. The remedy for Phil's rigidity, for his drive to find the "right" way to control his compulsivity, is the healthy giving up of control we know as conversion. It is the real remedy for Phil's shame. Shame constitutes an unbearable burden. It is a double-cross blocking the way to forgiveness and spawning numbing behaviors rather than surrender. Phil, in fact each one of us who aspires to serve in the image of Christ, must find another way, the way of conversion. That way is open in the *communio* of the church, at least if we do not close it to each other.

Hecker, Trepper, Wetchler, and Fontaine conducted a study that indicated how assessments might be skewed by the religiosity and gender of the therapists who conducted them.[17] One hundred and ninety-nine persons of the four hundred randomly selected members of AAMFT who were asked to respond did so. The results are interesting.

The therapists tended to assess single persons as more pathological than married persons who were assessed. Male therapists tended to see more pathology in clients overall than female therapists. The more highly religious the therapist the more the counselor was prone to judge as addictive the behaviors of the clients. This was especially true of male therapists who were highly religious. Overall, the therapists tended to make these judgments about the pathological tendencies they claimed to see on the basis of criteria that are not recognized as appropriate for assessment of addiction but are nonetheless socially operative. For instance, whether a married woman was faithful to her husband, while showing other signs of sex addiction, was judged as a counter indicative of addiction. The study functions to warn clinicians and non-clinicians that the level of religious practice of the assessor, as well as the gender, may influence the assessment. Seminary formators are not clinicians. However, they may be just as prone to see more pathology than is warranted in the person who has come to them for help.

Nicholas Abraham in his review of the literature on addiction and its relationship with religious messages indicates that "available research to date has established religion's potential to foster either positive or negative mental health."[18] He concludes,

> the relationship between delusional thought processes (core beliefs) and religious thought processes (religious beliefs) will be a significant area for exploration once an understanding of religious thought processes had become more advanced…. The debate among addictionologists, however important it is to setting appropriate standards and agreed-upon definitions, challenges researchers to develop a standardized formulation for the observation and description of religious messages received by people who engage in sexually addictive behavior.[19]

Seminaries are schools of religious messages—not just those to be repeated for the sake of the faithful after ordination, but messages to be heard as formation by seminarians, men who will be sent to hand on the faith. With attention to the literature on sexual addiction, it is possible to offer messages that will form men for the priesthood who themselves will be living witnesses to conversion, reconciliation, and *communio* in the church.

Reverend Richard Chiola, Ph.D., a priest of the Diocese of Springfield in Illinois, taught pastoral theology at Yale Divinity School and St. John's University, Collegeville. He currently is a certified sexual addiction therapist; administers St. Augustine Parish in Ashland, Illinois; and offers spiritual direction and pastoral counseling in Springfield.

Notes

1. Patrick J. Carnes, *Facing the Shadow: Starting Sexual And Relational Recovery* (Scottsdale, AZ: Gentle Path Press, 2001), p. 269.
2. The most available and helpful source is Patrick Carnes' twenty-year-old classic, *Out of the Shadows,* now in its third edition. (*Out of the Shadows: Understanding Sexual Addiction.* Hazelden, 2001.)
3. Patrick Carnes, *Contrary to Love* (Hazelden), pp. 61-68.
4. Patrick Carnes, "Sexual Addiction and Compulsion: Recognition, Treatment, and Recovery," *CNS Spectrums*, vol. 5, no. 10 (October 2000), p. 65.
5. Patrick Carnes, *Don't Call It Love: Recovery from Sexual Addiction* (Bantam Books, 1991), pp. 42-44.
6. Mark Laaser, *Faithful and True: Sexual Integrity in a Fallen World* (Zondervan Publishing House, 1996), p. 48.
7. Gerald May, *Care of Mind, Care of Spirit: a Psychiatrist Explores Spiritual Direction* (Harper San Francisco, 1992).
8. Kurt Stasiak, OSB, *A Confessor's Handbook* (Paulist Press, 1999), pp. 7-23.
9. Patrick Carnes, *Out of the Shadows: Understanding Sexual Addiction* (Hazelden, 2001), pp. 107-115.
10. Karl Rahner, SJ, "Guilt and Its Remission: The Borderline between Theology and Psychotherapy," chap. 9 in *Theological Investigations, Vol II*, (Helicon Press, 1963), p. 271.
11. Patrick Carnes, *Out of the Shadows: Understanding Sexual Addiction* (Hazelden, 2001).
12. Eli Coleman, "Compulsive Sexual Behavior: What to call it, How to treat it?" *Siecus Report*, vol. 31,

no. 5 (July-August 2003), pp. 12-16. Jim Orford, *Excessive Appetites: A Psychological View of Addictions* (2nd edition) (West Sussex, England: John Wiley & Sons Ltd., 2001). J. Money, *Lovemaps: Clinical Concepts of Sexual Erotic Health and Pathology, Paraphilia, and Gender Transposition in Childhood, Adolescence, and Maturity* (New York: Irvington, 1998), as cited in Wolfe, 2000.

13. Joe Kort, *Cass Model of Gay & Lesbian Identity Formation*, 2003, www.joekort.com. Adapted from Vivienne C. Cass, "Homosexual Identity Formation: A Theoretical Model," in *Journal of Homosexuality*, vol. 4, no. 3 (Spring 1779), and Betty Berzon, *Permanent Partners*, (New York: Penguin Books, 1988).

14. Patrick Carnes, *Contrary to Love: Helping the sexual Addict* (Center City, MN: Hazelden, 1989), p. 228.

15. David Delmonico and Elizabeth Griffin. "Classifying Problematic Sexual Behavior: a Working Model," chap. 23 in Patrick Carnes and Kenneth Adams, eds, *Clinical Management of Sex Addiction* (Great Britain: Brunner-Routledge, 2002), p. 361.

16. Patrick Carnes, and Marie Wilson, "The Sexual Addiction Assessment Process," chap. 1 in Patrick Carnes and Kenneth Adams, eds, *Clinical Management of Sex Addiction* (Great Britain: Brunner-Routledge, 2002), p. 13.

17. Lorna L.Hecker, Terry S. Trepper, Joseph L. Wetchler, and Karen L. Fontaine, "The Influence of Therapist Values, Religiosity and Gender in the Initial Assessment of Sexual Addiction by Family Therapists," *The American Journal of Family Therapy*, vol. 23, no. 3 (Fall 1995), pp. 261-272.

18. W. Nicholas Abraham, "The Significance of Religious Messages in Sexual Addiction: A Literature Review," *Journal of Sexual Addiction and Compulsivity*, vol. 1, no. 2, p. 163.

19. Ibid., p. 180.

In a Plain Brown Wrapper: Help For The Sex Addict

Stephen Olert, FSC, and Ruthann Williams, OP

This article is reprinted from Seminary Journal, *Volume 9, Winter 2003.*

Scene: a dinner party anywhere in "liberated" America. The 12 people gathered are young or old or somewhere in between. There is much laughter. Conversation has run the gamut. There is a recovering alcoholic...and everyone knows. They've discussed it, even. And it's okay. There's a member of Overeaters Anonymous...and everyone knows. That's okay too. There's a gay couple. Also okay. Five of the twelve smoke. Three are into "recreational" drugs. Okay. There are also present a few workaholics, a gambler, and an obsessive shopper. Okay, Okay.

Addictions of every kind and description are named and accepted. Almost, even, chic. We are, after all, a tolerant society, and "whatever turns you on" is certainly okay. But is it really?

Statistically, and the statistics are still young, one out of the 12 is another kind of addict. An unnamable, secret, hidden addict. One who cannot speak out because if he/she did the scene would change rapidly to one person, isolated, locked in a private hell and convinced that there is no help, no understanding to be had. That person is a sexual addict, a sexaholic.

The sex addict exists. In numbers greater than most of us imagine. It is the purpose of this article to call attention to this fact, to describe some of the symptoms so that the addiction can be recognized, and to suggest a plan—combining

> ## "Is this it? Have I been discovered? Is this the end of everything I've worked for, dreamed of?"

the practical and the spiritual—by which sexual addiction can be treated.

The sex addict exists. That addict is not limited to the single, the married, the religious, the ordained, the heterosexual, or the homosexual life style. We must confront and accept that fact. Controlled by a compulsion that is larger than any simple act of self will, the sex addict finds her/himself caught in a world one addict described as "hell as it is." She continued, "I was so alone and so ashamed. I think that must be what hell is really like. Total aloneness. And guilt and shame. With no hope of any way out. Ever."

Sexual compulsions are not limited to the rapist or the nymphomaniac, but are as varied as the people who are imprisoned in them. Whether it is masturbation or voyeurism or exhibitionism or incest, the compulsion grips the individual and frequently is as inexorably death producing as alcoholism or other chemical dependencies.

Forced into Hiding

Whatever the sexual compulsion, it results in behavior which is strongly disapproved of, even condemned, by our society, our culture, and our church. So the sexually compulsive person is forced into hiding, running, searching, fearing, but only rarely into hoping.

The sexaholic feels enormous shame and guilt, regardless of his or her state of life. "What I am doing is wrong. No one can understand or forgive me." It is a very short step then to the belief that not even God can forgive. The despair and isolation become more intense, and the sexaholic continues to act out the compulsion.

There is a constant and increasing threat of exposure. Every police siren, every ring of the telephone become potential dangers. Is this it? Have I been discovered? Is this the end of everything I've worked for, dreamed of? Marriage, career, religious community, priesthood, friends, family? The sexaholic becomes paranoid in his or her anxiety not to be found out.

There is usually a growing lack of ability to stop the behavior once and for all. Each acting out, each breaking over the boundaries of what desired behavior is, pushes the sexaholic further into self-hatred. In desperation the sexual addict vows to get under control, to become "normal." However, the compulsion invariably has its way, leaving the addict spent, guilt-ridden, and very alone.

In this helpless cycle the individual feels that no one can possibly understand his problem. He may recognize that he needs help but has no idea where to turn. He doubts that anyone else has ever experienced this kind of agony. Sometimes, if his desperation becomes great enough, he attempts suicide. Unfortunately, he often succeeds.

The other side of that desperation sees the addict convince himself that with a supreme effort of will he can get himself under control, that he can outwit this cunning and powerful compulsion. He fights against it with all his might, changing companions, jobs, leisure activities, even spouses in his efforts. He becomes rigid and unspontaneous and ever more deeply troubled. There is no joy in his life.

Or she feels a false sense of confidence and bolsters herself into believing that she can live in the face of the disapproval of society and the church. She "doesn't care" what anybody thinks. She'll live as she pleases and to hell with the rest

of the world. She stops struggling and yields to the compulsion with abandon in the hope that somehow the urges will be appeased. The security of "love," over and over again. There is less satisfaction, more guilt. The cycle continues and becomes slavery. The sex addict lives in a world of angry shame.

> **"New sensations and new relationships are canvassed in an attempt to find a synthetic substitute for love."**

If you can, imagine for a few moments that you are thirsty, incredibly and undeniably thirsty. Your dryness has gone beyond your mouth and has spread throughout your entire body. You have drunk all the pure, fresh water available. But your thirst, your dreadful, insatiable thirst continues. All that's left to drink is unwholesome water, alive with germs and evil bacteria. But it is water and you are thirsty. You try to resist it. You say to yourself that you can resist it. You will to resist it. But you are so, so thirsty. The water glitters before you, tempting. You turn your back on it, determined that you will not drink it. You won't. But what if it vanishes? What if the thirst gets worse and the water has somehow dried up? What if you are left with nothing but thirst? You cannot remove from your consciousness the thought of that cool, wet water. And so you give in. You gulp it down, eagerly, desperately, loving the way the wetness feels on your lips, your tongue, your throat. You drink and drink uncontrollably. At last you are satisfied.

Addiction's Elements

But it was not wholesome water. Your stomach turns and you are sick with a sickness that matches the intensity of your earlier desire. You are sick. And then you are thirsty again and you begin to seek more water. You become thirstier and thirstier.

You have now entered the world of the compulsed addict. You have experienced in imagination the three elements that constitute an addiction.

1. You have felt an overpowering need.
2. You have been frightened at the possible absence of a way of gratifying that need.
3. You have given in to the need even while knowing that the satisfaction was only temporary.

To these we would add a fourth:

4. The overpowering need returns.

As we have just indicated, compulsive sexual behavior only temporarily reduces the anxiety which usually stems from low self esteem, loneliness, fear of intimacy, fear of failure, rejection, and inability to cope with the world. Please notice also that compulsive sexual behavior tends to reinforce those causes once the peak moment of gratification is past. The anxiety returns, the belief that the addict just cannot contend with reality. The individual accumulates more guilt and, consequently, more of a need to escape into acting out.

Main Concern

The sex addict may act out at any one of several planes. The first includes masturbation, heterosexual and homosexual relationships of a compulsive nature, pornography, and prostitution. The next plane incorporates exhibitionism, voyeurism, indecent phone calls, and indecent liberties. Child molestation, incest, and rape make up the bulk of the third plane. Obviously the sexual addict at the first plane is considered "less dangerous" to society than one at the third plane. But our concern here is not society's reaction but rather the acute pain and frustration of the addict, regardless of the plane at which he or she is acting out. An addiction to peppermint is certainly viewed as less harmful than an addiction to heroin, but it is important to remember that the compulsion is no less real.

It is not unknown for a sex addict to progress from one plane to the next as the need for complete and final gratification escalates. From masturbation to voyeurism to cruising is not a long journey. New sensations and new relationships are canvassed in an attempt to find a synthetic substitute for love.

Temporary Realism

The sexaholic in his quiet moments denies the meaning of his behavior, lies, expects miracles, wishes he were dead, and prays for release. But when he changes into his secret identity, he becomes powerful. He feels in control even though the reverse is true, for in his acting out he does not need to lie about his feelings. It is possible that the fantasy even becomes the reality, becoming more actual to the addict than the remainder of his life. He is lost in time and space, transported. The names he makes up, the roles he takes on, the clothes he wears have a kind of desperate honesty about them. They are designed to release his truth. They allow him to be real.

But the realism is temporary. The normal world reasserts itself. The sex addict scurries back into the life in which she pretends that everything is fine. Unfortunately, she carries back with her an increasingly heavy bag of guilt, self-loathing, fear, and despair. Only in fantasy, in moments of acting out, is this bag laid aside.

> ## "If willpower alone is enough, the person is not suffering from a compulsion."

For the Christian there is added personal pain and suffering. Striving to incorporate Christian values into her life, she finds herself in constant conflict with her sexual behavior. This creates increased anxiety (with the resultant increased acting out) which becomes another obstacle to a trusting and loving relationship with God. At times this raw, unbearable suffering leaves her torn between her never-quenched sexual desire and an equally never-quenched longing to be at one with God.

Pain becomes the addict's home. And there is fear of moving out of this to the unknown, however promising it may seem. Lost in the confusing maze of his sexual dilemma and his Christian conscience, tense and angry, the sex addict is full of self-disgust. And the defeating, defeated cycle continues.

Hopefully, the sexaholic comes to the end of his rope before he is discovered and his worst fears are realized. He becomes sick and tired of being sick and tired. He admits he has a problem over which he has no control. He has exhausted his own resources. He is willing to make any change in order to end his compulsion.

At this point the sex addict accepts that the problem is within himself. He accepts the fact that his behavior is slavery. He stops and faces reality with a willingness to recognize the internal nature of his problem. So long as the problem remains "out there," he will make no genuine effort toward improvement. But coming to this realization is not easy. The descent to the bottom of one's resources is a bruising and painful experience. The ascent requires patience, perseverance, determination, and help. In many cases, when understanding help is available he will be able to make the ascent and find himself healed and whole, always a sexaholic, but a recovering and joyful one.

The emotional problems of the compulsive personality are the same, whether the compulsions involve alcohol, food, or sex. Willpower, the desire to change, counseling, and God are necessary to come to peace and health. If willpower alone is enough, the person is not suffering from a compulsion. This is the distinguishing line which separates ordinary sexual tension from compulsive sexual addiction.

It is an unfortunate—more, it is a deadly—fact that too often the sex addict seeking help runs into disgust and a complete lack of understanding. He is told that people who do "things like that" are sinners, simply lacking in will-power. So the addict goes back to his unhappy life, not knowing that his will alone cannot control the compulsion. Nor does he know that the compulsion is not the real problem, but only a symptom of inner emotional disturbances that must be healed before the symptoms will begin to decrease. When the sources of the compulsion have been found and named, the person can straighten out her life, provided she is willing to revise her thinking. No one is capable of changing her basic patterns of feeling unless she wants this change more than anything else in the world. Even then, counseling, a support group, and spiritual direction are necessary.

Assistance Needed

Those who have not suffered from compulsive behavior may not be able to recognize the difference between habit and compulsion and, consequently, may not be able to comprehend the agony and helplessness suffered by those who are caught in the clutches of such a symptom. Too often the unafflicted say that normal living is simply a matter of will. They do not know how often the individual suffering from a compulsion has told himself the very same thing. Compulsive behavior hits the strong, the weak, the rich, the poor, the educated, and the uneducated. It is no respecter of persons, and is certainly no respecter of the vowed religious, ordained or non-ordained. Compulsive sexual behavior is so strong that it cannot be controlled—without assistance—despite its destructive consequences. It is a fix, a physical need as powerful as the need for alcohol or drugs or oxygen. It is vital to recognize it as a need, not just a wayward desire.

In coming to a resolution about compulsive sexual behavior, the sex addict must acknowledge that it has to be finished. Completely. As the recovering alcoholic knows that there is no such thing as "just one" little drink, so the sexaholic must realize that there can be no occasion of "just one" little acting out. There are no half-measures for the addict. There is only cold turkey. But it need not, in fact must not, be handled alone. Personal change and conversion are done in the company of others and God. In this way it becomes possible for the person to take her inner life seriously, to face her deepest conflicts, and to conquer the monsters that lurk within.

For the sexaholic to free himself from a compulsion is to admit that it exists and that its presence is an uncontrollable factor in his life. It is very hard to admit to this reality. Those with sexual compulsions must come to a realization that ordinary methods of control will not work and that there is something basically out of step with the self which makes this area of life unmanageable.

When one takes the beginning steps toward recovery, he is saying that this compulsion is evidence that his whole way of life is out of control. Along with this admission must come a

> ### "They only disappear gradually as one increasingly develops a realignment of basic needs and basic ways of satisfying those needs."

growing understanding of why his particular personality needs to maintain the compulsion as a balance wheel. Sexual compulsions are not removed by resigning from the world. They only disappear gradually as one increasingly develops a realignment of basic needs and basic ways of satisfying those needs. Healing and growth do not take place in those who are unwilling to face the pain of "working through" their problems and who refuse to tolerate apparent regression in order to progress.

With the acknowledgement that there is a problem and the sincere desire for change, healing will occur when the individual has the time to rest, to gather herself in, and to admit that help needs to be sought. Only then will she be ready to be healed. The result of the inner struggle she experiences is a resolution to reform her life. For every step she will take toward liberation, she will in some way have to start over again. One is made and remade. In fact, her becoming fully human depends on her willingness to respond to God's challenge to be more than she thinks she is. A beginning is always difficult. The addict does not have to feel differently to act differently, but must keep in mind that she is never finished dealing with the depths of her inner life. Ignorance, reservation, dishonesty, and indifference can hold her back. She must be wholeheartedly willing to be "made new." It is not enough just to alter the symptom. The disease itself must be attacked.

Single-Issue Program

A necessary ingredient of any plan for a compulsive personality is a recovery program. A good recovery program, such as Sexaholics Anonymous, will work if the addict will follow it. Sexaholics Anonymous, like Alcoholics Anonymous, follows a twelve-step program to recovery, beginning with the admission that the addict is powerless over lust and working through to dependence on God, acknowledgement of wrongdoing, prayer and meditation, and finally a sort of "missioning" in which the SA member agrees to try to carry a redemptive message to other sex addicts. SA is a "single issue" organization, involved only in helping sexaholics to stay "sober." Its strength seems to lie in its spiritual foundation and its peer ministry. It is a dying to self and a rising to new life, in turn leading to helping others. It is a "gift given as gift," one of the best programs available for the Christian sexaholic.

There are no simple solutions, but if the sex addict sincerely desires sobriety, organizations such as SA can help. The addict must acquire honesty, humility, and appreciation and must be willing to kill self-centeredness in order to stay sober.

Spirituality Important

A good recovery program will enable the individual to become more aware of who he is as opposed to who he thinks he is. The program will help him to see incongruities between who he is and how he lives. It is a journey which involves grasping onto and then letting go of chunk after chunk of the old self.

Within every good recovery program is an important spiritual dimension. The individual knows that spiritual growth is a process. He begins by practicing how to do it, and then spends the rest of his life doing it, growing and changing as God leads and directs him. But it is not a victory easily won.

Along with this practical approach to help for the sexaholic, we believe that spiritual direction and/or pastoral counseling are necessary to round out the recovery program. For purposes of length our discussion will concern only the spiritual director, but everything that is said may be applied to the pastoral counselor as well.

The spiritual director, as in any direction situation, needs to be a friend to the sex addict: understanding, compassionate, gentle, and nonjudgmental. Ideally the spiritual director also has some knowledge of what sex addiction is and the particular effect it can have on the vowed religious who comes for help.

Necessary Four Steps

The spiritual director must be aware that occasional sin is not sex addiction. The addict's behavior is repetitive and compulsive. It probably interferes with his or her work responsibilities, at least on occasion. And it most certainly has had an impact on personal relationships. At the same time the director should be aware that there is help and hope for the sexually addicted. The director should become familiar with various recovery programs such as SA and should work with the individual toward the four steps necessary for recovery. First, the addict must admit his or her condition. Second, the acting out must be stopped. Next, the addict must be willing to do whatever is necessary to move toward recovery. Finally, he or she must be helped toward the long-range adjustment.

At the same time, the spiritual director must be conscious of his/ her own inner attitudes. The sex addict will look to the director to be a fellow journeyer along the path to recovery. It is not possible to companion someone who is held in contempt. Consequently, the spiritual director is called upon to practice Christianity to the fullest extent, wanting only good for the directee no matter how repugnant the information revealed might be.

Critical Role

The sexually compulsed person comes to the spiritual director with an attitude of inner evil, of unworthiness, guilt, and self pity. It is important that the director bring to the fore, in whatever manner seems most appropriate, the reality of God's unconditional love and acceptance of the person as he or she is.

The sex addict looks to the director for help in coming to see the movement of the Spirit in his or her life. It is vital to listen carefully, for the Spirit cannot be tamed into acting only in certain ways or at certain times. But the very fact that the sex addict has come for help is indication that the Spirit is working.

At this point in the addict's life, the role of the spiritual director is critical to further the desire

to change, to facilitate the conversion. The individual who chooses to allow the Lord to work in his or her life cannot remain unchanged. This change may not be a dramatic conversion, but the experienced director will be able to sense the longing of the heart person to change and to focus on the Lord. Every impulse in his body is toward Jesus, even though it may take years to overcome the fantasies and compulsive/addictive tendencies and cravings.

Gentleness Needed

Helping the person to have a grasp on the movement of good and evil and the role and value of the consciousness examen will be invaluable in the direction process. It is as important to learn to recognize the positive and powerful activity of God in a life as it is to recognize the evil.

Gentleness on the part of the spiritual director is necessary to help the individual move from beating herself to accepting herself as one whom God loves. This ambiance will allow the Spirit to surface for her those things that are neither good nor pleasant. With understanding and support, the addict needs to face the darkness within so that God's light may become hers. In walking with the sexually addicted person, it is essential that the spiritual director never communicate disappointment with the behavior of the directee. Rather, the director should travel with the person and discover in the heart of weakness the compassion, love, and presence of God.

Perhaps the key for the spiritual director is not so much an attitude of "there, but for the grace of God, go I" as "there, with the grace of God, go we all."

Stephen Olert, FSC, a member of the New York Province of the De La Salle Christian Brothers, is currently assistant provincial and director of formation. bsofsc@hotmail.com

Ruthann Williams, OP, is the communications manager for Sacred Heart Southern Missions, headquartered in Walls, Mississippi.

Recommended Reding

Carnes, Patrick. *Out of the Shadows.* Minneapolis, MN: CompCare Publications, 1983.

Groeschel, Benedict, OFM Cap. *The Courage to be Chaste.* Ramsey, NJ: Paulist Press, 1985.

In preparation for the 2004 Seminary Convocation, Michael Morton, director of educational training for Guest House, developed a series of case studies that represented the complexity of addiction issues and situations formation personnel are likely to encounter. (See pages 64-69.) They provided a context for the following panel interaction.

If I Knew Then: From the Perspective of a Family Therapist

Michael Morton, L.M.F.T.

This article is reprinted from Seminary Journal, *Volume 10, Fall 2004.*

The case studies presented at the Boston meeting for response and discussion were based upon a variety of men's histories entering treatment for alcoholism and other addictions and emotional problems either during seminary or after ordination at various ages. Some were surprised by the severity of the symptoms and complicated problems evidenced in the cases. Asked to respond from the perspective of a family therapist, I was caught by the trauma before entering seminary in certain stories, as well as the extent of the progression of the addictive illness before intervention.

One would like to think there is a way to discern or predict the viability of candidates for ministry, considering the physical, emotional, and spiritual aspects of addictive disorders and the manifest signs in the cases reviewed. The inevitable questions are asked: "How could these individuals be detected or identified at an earlier stage?" and "How does the illness progress to the chronic and destructive stages without some recognition or intervention?" I will summarize what might be part answer and part solution to the above realities as they surface in individuals in each generation of candidates for ministry.

Common to our culture today is the reality of men struggling with the effects of traumatic events in their lives and in the lives of others. We live in a culture with a high incidence of social problems such as abuse, neglect of children, poverty, physical, and emotional problems. Many men are raised in families troubled by issues as divorce, infidelity, addiction, and so on. In a developmental framework such "survivors" may learn to mask problems. These same problems come to light later in life, frequently under circumstances of extreme stress. In the meanwhile there are numerous ways to manage or medicate emotional pain and illness. The list of behaviors and substances for abuse is lengthy and many can be contained or denied for decades.

> ## "The most significant psychological defense mechanism in the addictive process is denial."

The most significant psychological defense mechanism in the addictive process is denial. This denial acts in such a manner as to attribute problems to something other than the addiction in order not to have to face the pain of forgoing the pleasure or relief given by the behavior or substance.

Addiction as an illness is defined as primary, progressive, chronic, and potentially fatal. It is also understood to have a major impact upon those involved in the addict's life. In my experience this is so much the case that many are at a great disadvantage to address addiction due to the traumatizing aspects of the problem. In a sense we are left "speechless."

The rules for the addictive family are several. They include silence, rigidity, denial, and isolation. The norm is "Don't talk. Don't trust. Don't feel. Don't touch." The institutions and systems that "Adult Children" enter are frequently governed by rules that are similar to those mentioned above. The rules help to reinforce the addictive process rather than challenge or unmask it. I think seminaries and presbyterates need to encourage the alternative rules where trust, dialogue, and expression of emotions are encouraged.

The system within which the candidate for priesthood navigates must exhibit the health and normative features of a spiritually, emotionally, and physically healthy family. The health of the family will address the illness or problems in the individual members and have an appropriate discernment process when problems are identified. This would call for living consciously and in communion with others. The rules would encourage confidence in the integrity of the culture, hence an openness to talk, trust, and feel when to do so is a healthy expression of conscious and committed living.

Basic understanding of the nature of addiction and its many faces and processes are prerequisites for action when addiction shows itself in individuals. A well-developed and enforced policy regarding the various addictions and compulsions, including elementary information such as signs and symptoms, is important. Steps to resolve possible concerns within the context of the seminary and clearly spelled-out responsibilities and roles for all involved are vital to the effectiveness of the policy. Appropriate education of staff, faculty, and students with a clear understanding of consequences for violation of the policy can be a help to prevention as well as early intervention. Last, but most important, the faculty and staff must be held to the same standard to which they are holding the seminarians. Any compromise in authority will result in a compromised ability to deal effectively with the seminarians.

Michael Morton, L.M.F.T., is an educator, trainer, and therapist with over 30 years experience in helping individuals, institutions, and families. He enjoys a national reputation presenting and training professionals, organizations, and groups with special needs. Mr. Morton was the director of a national unit for sexual addiction and a former board member of the National Council for Sexual Addiction and Compulsivity. He is a clinical member of the American Association of Marriage and Family Therapists and a licensed Family Therapist. Presently he is the director of education and training for Guest House.

Psychological Perspectives, Addiction, and Formation Issues

Kevin P. McClone, M.Div., Psy.D.

This article is reprinted from Seminary Journal, *Volume 10, Fall 2004.*

I have been asked to focus my comments on the psychological dynamics and vulnerabilities that were present in the various cases discussed. In reflecting on the psychological vulnerabilities, it was clear that in most of the cases, alcohol and other substances or behaviors were used to relieve *"emotional discomfort."* Indeed, a characteristic pattern of the addictive process is when underlying fears, anxieties, and loss are not faced directly but denied through addictive behaviors that seek to mask the pain. Addicts' feelings of inferiority often get soothed through the addictive behavior, where they can feel successful at least for a time, albeit temporary and illusory. It allows people to self-medicate and anesthetize their loneliness, alienation, and fears, finding some temporary solace, relief, and peace.

Another pattern I saw reflected in the various cases discussed was the progressive nature of the addictive process from gradual use to out of control patterns of use and abuse. Addicted persons rarely become addicted all at once but rather gradually over many years, and often with some period of prolonged abstinence. The addicted person is often the master of leading a double life and does so most effectively when others remain at a distance. Indeed, in some of the cases there was clear knowledge that some drinking problem

> **"Those communities and formation personnel who model an environment of openness, honesty, and accountability will be better equipped to deal with addictive patterns."**

existed, and yet intervention didn't occur until much later in the process. I recall one seminarian telling me of an older member of his community who clearly had a problem with alcohol abuse, but the community seemed either to just joke about it or to avoid confronting the person, and he felt a subtle pressure to maintain the denial. Since the addict thrives on living an isolated existence, communities and formation personnel who are genuinely caring, curious, and courageous enough to confront unhealthy patterns will be the most effective in unmasking the denial.

Indeed, despite what seemed to be obvious problems and negative consequences from drinking or other addictive patterns, the priests and seminarians in the case studies didn't see the nature of their problem. In many cases the community and significant others in the addict's life were also in various states of denial. Clearly there is need for more education and awareness concerning the dynamics of addictions. Those communities and formation personnel who model an environment of openness, honesty, and accountability will be better equipped to deal with addictive patterns.

Another key dynamic reflected in the case studies of the priests and seminarians discussed was the presence of shame-based histories. Looking at the family of origin data of addicted persons, one sees a familiar pattern of an internalized sense of shame, often as an outgrowth of a more heavy-handed authoritarianism growing up. In fact, in one major study this factor—often referred to as *"irrational authoritarianism,"* meaning authority based mostly on superior power—was present in three fourths of family histories of the alcoholics studied. Many of these psychological vulnerabilities cause wounded individuals and family systems that experience high alienation as well as anxiety, shame, and low self esteem and general well being. These factors cause them to be hyper vulnerable to becoming addictive if addictive substances are used or addictive behaviors begun. Early intervention and treatment of addictive patterns will be more likely when such vulnerabilities are recognized. Models of healthy authority in formation that are even-handed and balanced will be of great assistance to the addicted person.

Many have written about the relationship between shame and addiction. This is especially evident in sexual addiction, where Patrick Carnes notes that some of the core beliefs of the sexual addict are "I am a bad an unworthy person," and "No one could possible love me for who I am." This shame has its roots in family-of-origin history and gets played out in religious who may be superacheivers who feel driven and are unable to find emotional balance. Shame-based histories of alcoholics and children of alcoholics leads to a fear of punishment, the perception of God as punisher, and the feeling that I'm not worthy and deserving of love. Past deeds haunt the person, so recovery is all about mercy, compassion, and forgiveness. The antidote to shame is an atmosphere of acceptance, tolerance, and forgiveness rooted in genuine concern for the recovery of the addicted person.

Another psychological theme is *"perfectionism."* This is often found in clergy and religious who struggle with addictive patterns. Unrealistic expectations beginning in childhood and often reinforced through spiritual pursuits of perfection set one up for failure by having unrealistic goals that can't be attained. They eventually lead to self-punishing guilt and shame. False pride often can become a wall behind which the addict hides. It is necessary to give up the search for perfection.

Healthy formation in the context of an additive society will challenge us to develop more comprehensive and practical assessment measures that focus on healthy psychosexual development, affective maturity, and building healthy relationships. Many of the cases highlighted the emotional and psychosexual immaturity that underlined many of the persons struggling with addictive patterns. Sometimes reflected in poor interpersonal relationships or struggles with intimacy and authority, this underlying sexual immaturity contributed to the addicted persons' vulnerability. What seemed clear in the patterns of the cases was the need for deeper awareness at all three levels of prevention: primary, secondary, and tertiary. In other words, developing programs for vocation and formation personnel that offer broad-based education, target at risk persons, and implement more effective relapse prevention strategies for those already struggling with addictions.

Kevin P. McClone, M.Div., Psy.D., is a licensed clinical psychologist, certified alcohol and drug counselor, and certified chaplain who has worked for more than 20 years in the health care field.

Factors that Influence a Seminarian's Understanding of Substance Use and Abuse

Rev. Thomas F. Nestor

This article is reprinted from Seminary Journal, *Volume 10, Fall 2004.*

There are several important factors, among many, that influence the seminarian's understanding of substance use and abuse. The first is the culture in which he learned about substances. The second is the seminarian's psychological make-up, namely his personality structure, defense style, and coping skills. The third factor is the climate of priestly formation.

The first factor is a crucial and familiar one. The impact of the family's attitude toward alcohol, not to mention what in some cases is a genetic predisposition to alcoholism, is often the most obvious one. One is never surprised when alcohol abuse is found in people whose parents and siblings abuse alcohol. Some see such patterns repeating themselves over several generations as evidence of either an inherited allergy to alcohol that leaves the individual unable to drink in moderation or a family system problem that supports the abuse of alcohol.

Just as important, however, is the peer culture that has formed a seminarian's attitude toward, and use of, alcohol. The peer group is a major influence in adult development during late teens and the twenties. This young adult culture is saturated with alcohol abuse. In this culture, drunkenness is morally neutral and the only responsibility one has is not to drive a car while

> **"In this culture, drunkenness is morally neutral and the only responsibility one has is not to drive a car while under the influence of alcohol."**

under the influence of alcohol. Consuming five or six beers in the course of an evening is considered moderation, if not virtual abstinence! Moderation and abstinence require an explanation for one's peers as to why one is not drinking, while passing out or blacking out requires no explanation. Binge drinking on the college campus has been well documented and widely reported in the press.

If seminarians have not been involved in the excessive consumption of alcohol associated with college life and early adulthood, they have certainly been exposed to it. In this system, drinking, if not drunkenness, is a legitimate activity or end in itself. Thus when seminarians "go out drinking," they are likely participating in an activity the norms for which have been set by their peers and not mature adults. Of course, some carry adolescent drinking patterns into adulthood. The standard by which they evaluate their drinking is that set by the heaviest drinkers.

This affords false assurance that their drinking is not problematic.

Seminary formation personnel are aware that the language used and the values upheld in a priestly formation program are different from those with which a new seminarian is familiar. For instance, when young men come into the seminary they develop a whole new understanding of sexuality and intimacy. They learn that the word "intimacy" does not refer to genital acts alone but connotes a quality of relationship and self-disclosure. The same approach may be necessary in helping seminarians understand that the responsible and morally correct use of alcohol goes beyond designating a driver. In addition, a seminarian would benefit from examining the culture that shapes his attitude toward, and use of, alcohol. Introducing a seminarian to the world of adult norms may require a new glossary for naming substance-related activities and formulating an ethic of responsibility.

The second factor, psychological make-up, is a complex matter. The case studies reveal some important personality issues and behaviors often found in substance abusers and addicts. Compulsivity and impulsivity, as well as difficulty in understanding and modulating affectivity, run through the stories of those who abuse substances and develop addictive behavior. Clearly, substances and addictive activities provide temporary and maladaptive soothing which the individual might otherwise be unable to summon. Through the use of substances, depressive feelings get a brief reprieve but only worsen with these methods of self-soothing. The lack of interpersonal skills and/or fear of one's feeling put some at considerable risk to resort to injurious means of getting comfort. These practices may date back to adolescence when age appropriate social anxiety was alleviated with alcohol. The development of relational skills is thereby impeded. The psychological make-up of the seminarian is a significant factor in how he appropriates the program of priestly formation in his own life.

The climate of the formation program itself is the third factor influencing the seminarian's approach to alcohol use and abuse. At issue is whether the seminary is structured in such a way as to help the seminarian establish honest relationships with advisors in which self-disclosure is encouraged. In the course of priestly formation, the seminarian who takes the formation task seriously is inevitably going to be confronted with himself. He is assisted in developing self-knowledge by studying his family, personal history, and relationships. He is encouraged to entrust his spiritual and emotional states, as well as the nature of his relationships, to his advisors in both the internal forum and the external forum, as appropriate.

> **"In the course of priestly formation, the seminarian who takes the formation task seriously is inevitably going to be confronted with himself."**

In this task of developing self-knowledge, a formidable hurdle to negotiate is fear. Like anybody, a seminarian may struggle with a fear of his true self and thus be reluctant to enter into relationships of trust with peers and advisors. Some of the case studies depict characters whose relational life is underdeveloped or who apparently do not know themselves and are not known by others. The defensive maneuvers are familiar. In order to avoid unpleasant effects and indeed the self, a seminarian may resort to intellectualization and/or repression, to name only two. His intellectual abilities and emotional control may appear to be virtues, but they are not necessarily such if they are used to protect him from his emotional life. They are not oriented toward freedom and growth but toward developmental arrest and self-deception.

To live in such a prison with no communication with the true self is truly painful and isolating. The comfort afforded by alcohol, the escape provided by anonymous relationships, and the relief attained by a compulsive activity become overwhelmingly appealing. This "cure" does not work, of course, but the use of the "cure" for troubling feelings increases in frequency. The seminary is largely a predictable environment, while parochial life is not. The breakdown of these defenses is almost inevitable in the emotional demands of parochial ministry.

I have presented three factors related to addiction that I think merit careful consideration in preparing men for the priesthood. It behooves one in Holy Orders who aspires to be an expert in humanity to find in a priestly formation program the tools for maturation in human stature and freedom. Understanding what has shaped one's attitudes and behaviors, growth in self-awareness, and the freedom to address these matters in a trusting relationship with a formation advisor are important tasks for the seminarian and his advisors.

Rev. Thomas F. Nestor is a priest of the Archdiocese of Boston and a professor of psychology at St. John's Seminary in Brighton. He is also involved in the Human Formation Program at St. John's and the Office of Pastoral Support to Priests. In addition, Father Nestor serves as the administrator of St. Eulalia Parish in Winchester, Massachusetts.

Screening and Intervention with Personal Difficulties

Rev. Stephen J. Rossetti, Ph.D., D.Min.

This article is reprinted from Seminary Journal, *Volume 10, Fall 2004.*

In the wake of the sexual abuse crisis, there is a natural push for better screening of candidates for the priesthood. Certainly, there are ways the church can improve its screening and we should do everything possible. In fact, in the past twenty years there has been a noticeable improvement in the psychological screening and human formation of candidates for the priesthood. My experience has been that most dioceses and seminaries in this country are currently doing a fine job, and I think the upcoming apostolic visitation of our seminaries will bear this out.

However, we ought to be aware of the limitations of what psychological screening can do, especially in the area of sexual difficulties. Many times sexual pathology and addictions are hidden from view, perhaps even from the candidate. For example, when sexually troubled by serious inner conflicts and deviant attractions, people often repress and deny their desires. Most psychological testing will be largely ineffective in such cases.

What we at Saint Luke Institute have found works best for psychosexual screening is a thorough psychosexual history performed in a confidential setting by a licensed professional. In such a setting, there can be a sensitive inquiry

> **"The key to assisting seminarians as well as priests showing signs of difficulty is early intervention."**

with a view toward the presence, or absence, of a healthy psychosexual development and current sexual integration. While specific deviant development present in the candidate may not directly surface, a number of "red flags" and areas of concern often do. In this case, these areas can be the focus of future inquiry and formation.

Just as important as the initial screening is the ongoing screening of candidates throughout the formation process. The entire community ought to be alert to the surfacing of sexual difficulties and other deviant or addictive behaviors. There should be no hesitancy on the part of any, staff or seminarians, to bring attention to such difficulties in themselves or others.

This attitude of accountability ought to be carried over into the priesthood as well, as part of its ongoing formation. I remember well the case of an older priest who died after many years of being an active alcoholic. Other priests knew about his problem but said nothing. In the wake of the crisis, those days are over! Given all that has happened recently, we priests must be held accountable for our behaviors and given the necessary assistance when in need.

The key to assisting seminarians as well as priests showing signs of difficulty is early intervention. It is a tragedy when a long-overdue intervention takes place only as a seminarian enters the final stages of theology. At the first sign of difficulty, seminary formators are well advised not to overlook these budding signs. Rather, they ought to explore these signs and intervene at the earliest appropriate moment. Early intervention is an important key to dealing effectively with personal difficulties.

Initial and ongoing screening is an important key to forming a healthy presbyterate. But we ought to be aware of the limitations of such a human process. We will never screen out all the difficulties. Living with the messiness and human limitations of life is never easy.

Father Stephen J. Rossetti, Ph.D., D.Min., is a priest of the Diocese of Syracuse and licensed psychologist. Father Rossetti spent six years as an intelligence officer after graduating from the Air Force Academy in 1973. He holds a Ph.D. in psychology from Boston College, a Doctor of Ministry degree from The Catholic University of America, and is president and CEO of a residential treatment program for clergy and religious men and women. Father Rossetti wrote the bestseller, *I Am Awake*, as well as *Fire on the Earth* and *A Tragic Grace*.

Case Studies in Ministry Formation and Addictions

The following five case studies were selected by the panelists to represent the complexity of addiction issues and situations formation personnel are likely to encounter. They are included as a discussion resource, whether as part of a workshop for seminarians or an in-service program for faculty and staff.

This article is reprinted from Seminary Journal, *Volume 10, Fall 2004.*

Case #1

Father A was admitted for his first alcoholism treatment at age 42. He was discovered unconscious by parishioners who forced their way in to the rectory after no response to repeated attempts to contact him. He reported to the vicar for clergy the following day and was referred for evaluation before being admitted to residential treatment. He reported having a realization of his problem with alcohol and self-estimates a use of a half-gallon of vodka every three days.

Medically, Father A has an enlarged liver and impairment of liver functioning and elevated enzymes. He is being treated for heart problems and reports medication for high blood pressure.

He remembers his first consumption of alcohol at age 21. He reports sporadic use of alcohol that began in social situations with a gradual progression of use culminating in his recent consumption on a daily basis. His regular use was remembered at age 33 at which time he was drinking two beers daily and "perhaps four on Sunday." Within the present year he reports an escalation with drinking one gallon straight of Vodka per week and occasional beer, wine, and liqueurs.

He reported behavior changes and becoming more isolated, and "everything revolving around his drinking." He reported blackouts, some audio and visual hallucinations, and being physically fatigued with an inability to abstain from drinking. He reported the recent suicide of a close priest friend mentor as contributing to his increased use. He acknowledged use of alcohol to ward off withdrawal symptoms.

Father A was raised in a middle-class Protestant family and lost his father when he was 12 due to early death attributed to alcoholic drinking and depression. He reports having a good and loving relationship with his mother, who has remarried. His sister, age 46, is on good terms with him. She suffers from depression and is presently taking anti-depressant medication.

Father A converted to Catholicism at the age of 18 and almost immediately became interested in priesthood. After a year of college, he entered minor seminary at age 20. He went on to complete theology and was ordained at the age of 27.

During his first pastorate he reports taking an anti-depressant for a period of five years or so and being very anxious during this period. He remembers this helped him level his emotions but especially kept his anger in check. He remembers discontinuing use of the antidepressant, perhaps due to feeling better, perhaps due to his switching to alcohol.

While reporting no specific concerns about celibacy, sexuality, or previous relationships, at this time he reports being homosexual. Homosexuality was referred to as being "part of the human experience."

Of consequence is his father's premature death. While inebriated his father was killed in a fatal auto accident. His father was 43 at this time and Father A was 12. He appears to minimize the haunting circumstances of this tragedy and his present age and condition. His mother became employed and remarried two years latter when he was 14 years old. His mother and stepfather drank heavily but are presently drinking less. His parents are presently in their 70s.

> **"Other symptoms were insomnia, impaired appetite and a generalized slowing down in tempo, frequent feelings of inferiority, self-doubt about his level of confidence, while at the same time setting high standards for himself, and much self-blame for failure to live up to expectations."**

He reports that as a result of these experiences he had to grow up quickly and take on a good deal of responsibility for others. He reports maintaining the close relationship with his sister who is being treated for bipolar disorder. In his psychological assessment, he presented with high levels of distress indicating struggles with anxiety and depression. He also deals with a good deal of somatization of this distress such as tiredness, pains, and aches. Other symptoms were insomnia, impaired appetite and a generalized slowing down in tempo, frequent feelings of inferiority, self-doubt about his level of confidence, while at the same time setting high standards for himself, and much self-blame for failure to live up to expectations.

He presents a pattern of angry outbursts and impatience with others while feeling inadequate himself. He tends to isolate and withdraw from others in frustration and disappointment. He scores high as an introvert and shows a good deal of social discomfort, expressing a high degree of self-consciousness and intensity. His interpersonal fears are of intimacy and closeness due to fear of being rejected and ridiculed or shamed. While desiring friendships he drives others away and withdraws. His evaluation suggested long-term depression beginning from childhood, anxiety disorder with underlying obsessive-compulsive personality traits. He is organized, prompt, etc., with a degree of emotional repression and guardedness.

Case #2

Deacon B is a 34-year-old seminarian in his final year before ordination to the priesthood. He was admitted for treatment after his involvement in an automobile accident. He was charged with driving while intoxicated. He has two previous arrests for drunken diving and one previous conviction.

He was raised in a white upper-middleclass Catholic family. He has a younger brother and 2 sisters with whom he remains close. He denies any other addiction in the family and/or mental or emotional difficulties. He denies any major traumas or developmental issues during his formative years. His siblings have experienced academic success at higher levels.

He reports one intimate relationship after college and a period of sadness after the breakup of that relationship. He then had a spiritual awakening after this breakup that led to his desire for priesthood. He reports an active social life and sees himself as an extrovert with lots of dating experiences, which better qualifies him for knowing what a life of celibacy will entail.

Alcohol use began at the age 16 with reports of two to four beers per month. This progressed by age 23 to consuming five to eight mixed drinks at least five times per week until about age 29. During this period he worked in the restaurant/ entertainment business and attended college. Following graduation from college, he drank much less. He reported a use of about two to six drinks two times per week. His initial time at seminary the following year at age 30 involved a continued decrease in weekly drinking to about two to four beers or glasses of wine once per week and occasional binge drinking about three to five times per year. He also reports smoking pot during college.

He explained using alcohol to relieve emotional discomfort. Reported symptoms of use were increased tolerance, blackouts, withdrawal symptoms, complaints about use from others, loss of control when drinking, neglecting others, failing in his responsibilities, compromised values, becoming violent under the influence, being injured while in intoxicated, legal difficulties, and sexually acting out while under the influence.

He reports no other drug use and "only PRN medication for chronic back problems." No other medical issues were reported.

Psychological findings showed an above-average intelligence with intact thought processes and a clear comprehension of the effects of his drinking. There were no significant issues of anxiety or depression. However, data suggests issues around impulsivity and moments when he acts without thinking. His self-esteem and confidence seem largely intact. He appears very social and extroverted and accepted and approved of by others. He remains close to his family and friends. He exhibits no anti-social traits or cynicism and does not present any major authority conflicts.

Again, data suggests he tends to over control negative, hurt, or stressful feelings and it may well be that these emerge in times of alcohol use. He presently describes his stress around present conditions that may be situational due to legal and vocational risks pending. Interpersonally he comes across as a very affable, even charming individual who adheres to conventions and expectations. There is some indication of being a "free thinker" and may challenge the rules if he does not agree. However, his alcohol use is clearly a major problem with a lower-than-average addiction potential rating and concurrently an above-average response to the Addiction Acknowledgement Scale.

Case #3

Father C was 45 years old at time of admission for inpatient treatment following his first intervention and evaluation for alcohol use. He has been involved with AA off and on for years. This was part of his ongoing psychiatric

work when he became aware of his developing concerns about drinking. About two years prior to this admission he "surrendered" to more frequent use of alcohol. He remembers his use of alcohol in his teenage years and throughout much of his life, however periodic his use. He denies any other drug use other than some pot smoking in high school. He has known periods of abstinence and then relapsed. He acknowledges additional stressors at this time in his parish work and his parent's medical condition. He reports some relief at his referral for treatment.

Father C was born into a middle-class Catholic family, the second oldest in a family of five. His father was an educated professional. He is somewhat estranged from his oldest brother and closer to his younger siblings. His father committed suicide when Father C was in seminary. He had a history of depression and alcoholism. He reports his developmental history as one marked by denigration and of being shamed by his father. He relates ongoing issues with authority to these experiences of being shamed by his father. He has also struggled with sexual identity issues in outpatient treatment.

> **"Father C has been under psychiatric care for depression at least ten years and on a therapeutic regime of psychotropic medications, one a mood stabilizer, and sleeping medications. He reports sadness and a depressed mood going back to adolescence."**

Father C has been under psychiatric care for depression at least ten years and on a therapeutic regime of psychotropic medications, one a mood stabilizer, and sleeping medications. He reports sadness and a depressed mood going back to adolescence.

He was ordained at the age of 27, reporting difficulties in his first few assignments. At the beginning of his third year in ministry, he was on sick leave, followed by a formal leave of absence for the next two years. During this time he pursued other employment and was under psychiatric care for depression. He describes his present assignment as going well; however, he has intermittent conflicts with the pastor but attempts to handle these without running away. He considers his worst offences verbally abusing others.

Father C's evaluation revealed someone much afraid and anxious about himself and others. He reported very poor impulse control and was struggling at the time of evaluation with "staying in treatment." He reported his tendency to fight or take flight as ongoing. He acknowledges a problem of conflict between wanting to be close to others yet pushing them away.

Father C's intellectual abilities scored minimally at the average range, perhaps complicated by his present situation and protracted withdrawal. He describes himself as being trapped in intense emotions and fearing rejection and abandonment. Poor levels of self worth and esteem were evidenced in his concern about the approval of others, fear of being inadequate, and failing at task. He is basically unhappy most of the time and finds life to be a strain. In his own words he is high strung, restless, nervous, and tense and concerned about his future. His behavior can be erratic and volatile at times. Anger is an ongoing emotion and is directed outward at others.

He appears to be introverted and has difficulty meeting new people and being in new situations. As a result he remains emotionally distant from others although he desires more friendships. The problems with his father, struggles with authority, and issues with vocation are ongoing for Father C. He clearly expresses an awareness of the problems alcohol has created, a desire for sexual sobriety which he connects to abstinence from alcohol, a desire for right relationships with others, and purpose or the ability to make a difference.

Case #4

Father D was 51 years old when he was referred by concerned superiors for his first primary treatment for alcoholism. Contributing to their concerns was Father D's diabetes, hypertension, anxiety/panic disorder, gout, and obesity.

> **"In general father's drinking history is, at best, under-reported by him. He began drinking at age 18, with a graduated progression culminating in a minimum use of 1.5 gallons of liquor per week. "**

In general father's drinking history is, at best, under-reported by him. He began drinking at age 18, with a graduated progression culminating in a minimum use of 1.5 gallons of liquor per week. He denies any other illicit drug use although his anti-anxiety medication may be a cause for concern.

Father D entered minor seminary at age 15 and was ordained at age 23. The oldest of four children of modest income, he quickly became self-sufficient. His mother is deceased and his father, whom he visits often, is presently in a nursing care facility. Two of his siblings are on psychotropic medication for depression and/or anxiety. He was somewhat withholding about family history and denied any abuse in the family. His father is a recovering alcoholic with 20 years in recovery. No other major problems were reported.

Father D perceives himself as having been emotionally/mentally abused in ministry by a former pastor and housekeeper during a previous assignment. Otherwise he likes ministry and feels competent in his work, although he feels burdened by the demands from downtown for reports, etc.

Father D's psychological evaluation revealed a person with increasing stressors over the past 15 years involving increased workload, family illness, and an attempt to be present to the family. He explains increasing anxiety about his next assignment having a long-term position at his present church. Added to these issues are his chronic health problems.

His overall profile indicated anxiety and preoccupation with others' opinions about him and fear of criticism, with a strong need for approval and acceptance. He tends to blame and judges himself harshly for his defects. In spite of this he minimizes his problems and presents as being able to control things. In all he might be described as someone with a high degree of characterlogical anxiety and poor self-esteem with strong tendencies to control his emotions and handle things without help.

CASE #5

Seminarian E is 30 years old and in his second year of theology. Although he is performing well in his scholastic pursuits, he is reluctant to engage in many social activities and prefers to study in his room, doing the majority of his research online. While it is common for students to use the Internet for researching projects, he seems to do so more than the average student. His appearance in the morning is often tired and "frazzled," as one professor described him. The faculty is not in agreement as to his progress in all dimensions of priestly formation and there is disquiet among the formation team regarding his advancement. His spiritual director has raised issues with him numerous times regarding his struggle with relationships with others, as well as his growth toward a commitment to celibacy and chastity. Seminarian E has been discreet in speaking about his past history of romantic and sexual involvement, reporting a very firm commitment to his present life and a "worldly experience" which prepares him for the demands of celibacy.

Seminarian E was formerly employed in a corporate setting in a major urban center and attended a state university, majoring in economics and business management. He is the only child of parents who have remained married and he reports no major disruptions in his life or sexual, emotional, or physical abuse either in the home or anywhere outside of the home. He reports no issues relating to alcohol or other drugs. His parents, both still employed as professionals, appear to keep in contact with him and he maintains communication with a tight-knit group via email.

The seminary has hosted several workshops regarding cybersex and the Internet as well as compulsive behaviors and other addictions. Seminarian E has attended these conferences but retains a questioning and challenging response to issues of private access and privacy in general as he feels he is a mature adult. When it was suggested the seminary deny private use of the Internet and personal accounts, he organized a group to protest such a policy. He argued the universal use of the net and the inevitable need to learn to deal with its temptations in the real world.

In his meetings with his spiritual director, Seminarian E repeatedly brings issues of his struggle in dealing with lust and fantasy as well as a sense of dealing with some internal dissonance with his public and personal self. He is easily irritated with others and impatient, finds he spends too much time in his head, and lacks a sense of trust regarding self-disclosure even with his spiritual director. He sees himself as being moody and at times failing to be present for the needs of others as well as reluctant to participate in community life unless it involves using technology, especially computers and related devices. He is, for example, happy to research and develop Web sites, programs, brochures, etc., but quickly retreats from the accompanied socializing before or afterwards.

Maintaining confidentiality, Seminarian E's spiritual director sought outside professional consultation regarding concerns abut the possibility of compulsive cybersex activity, although he has no apparent means to check up on or demand an accounting of Seminarian E's online activity. The spiritual director has the intuitive sense there is "something" being withheld, hinted at, but not open to discussion, in the meetings with him. He likewise finds himself carrying the burden of his concerns under the obligation of confidentiality. The director has been seeking help in clarifying what might be indicators of a more serious problem, a means to invite Seminarian E to be more open, and a format within the seminary to openly discuss and deal with such issues as they emerge. He presently feels incapacitated within the existing structure to address the problem.

CORE COMPETENCIES FOR CLERGY AND PASTORAL MINISTERS IN ADDRESSING ALCOHOL AND DRUG DEPENDENCE AND THE IMPACT ON FAMILY MEMBERS

These competencies are presented as a specific guide to the core knowledge, attitudes, and skills which are essential to the ability of all clergy and pastoral ministers to meet the needs of persons with alcohol or drug dependence and their family members.

1. Be aware of the:
   - generally accepted definition of alcohol and drug dependence
   - societal stigma attached to alcohol and drug dependence

2. Be knowledgeable about the:
   - signs of alcohol and drug dependence
   - characteristics of withdrawal
   - effects on the individual and the family
   - characteristics of the stages of recovery

3. Be aware that possible indicators of the disease may include, among others: marital conflict, family violence (physical, emotional, and verbal), suicide, hospitalization, or encounters with the criminal justice system.

4. Understand that addiction erodes and blocks religious and spiritual development; and be able to effectively communicate the importance of spirituality and the practice of religion in recovery, using Scripture, traditions, and rituals of the faith community.

5. Be aware of the potential benefits of early intervention to the:
   - addicted person
   - family system
   - affected children

6. Be aware of appropriate pastoral interactions with the:
   - addicted person
   - family system
   - affected children

7. Be able to communicate and sustain:
   - an appropriate level of concern
   - messages of hope and caring

8. Be familiar with and utilize available community resources to ensure a continuum of care for the:
   - addicted person
   - family system
   - affected children

9. Have a general knowledge of and, where possible, exposure to:
   - the 12-step programs — AA, NA, Al-Anon, Nar-Anon, Alateen, ACOA, etc.
   - other groups

10. Be able to acknowledge and address values, issues, and attitudes regarding alcohol and drug use and dependence in:
    - oneself
    - one's own family

11. Be able to shape, form, and educate a caring congregation that welcomes and supports persons and families affected by alcohol and drug dependence.

12. Be aware of how prevention strategies can benefit the larger community.

(NACoA, 2003)

Addiction and Compulsive Behaviors: Identification and Intervention
A Guide for Ministers

Michael Morton, M.A., L.M.F.T.

Introduction

This resource is provided for those in positions of leadership who must deal with the impairment of those who are under their supervision and authority. It is not a clinical text nor a "how to" book. The materials are intended for the non-clinical person. The content is borrowed and developed from a series of presentations and lectures given to religious leadership as well as other resources created expressly for the purpose of education about the nature of addictive disorders.

The common requests from men and women in dealing with problems is, "How do I know or identify the problem? What are the related concerns? What do I do once I know that such is the case? Where do I turn for help? What happens once the person has sought help? What is my role in the recovery process? Is it sometimes the case that a person cannot return to work? What are the rights of the impaired person? Who else do I involve in the process and when?"

This following material will not answer all of the above concerns. In fact all the knowledge in the world does not necessarily translate into good practice. The booklet does enumerate basic principles, some specific suggestions, resources for help in the stages of the process, and a variety of tools for both the impaired other as well as

> **Topics to be covered in this manual:**
>
> - What You Don't Know Can Harm You
> - Barriers to Effective Supervision
> - The Nature of Addictive Disorders
> - Periodic Use and Abuse
> - Signs and Symptoms of Addiction
> - Identification & Intervention
> - Referral
> - Intervention
> - Religious Culture & Direct Address
> - Treatment and Recovery
> - Monitoring & Supervision

yourself in dealing with the stress of addiction and recovery.

The task of addressing problems in others and one's self is a complicated one fraught with potential pitfalls when undertaken alone or without proper backing from those with authority. This booklet is offered as a help in moving in the right direction.

What You Don't Know Can Harm You!

The title of this section (borrowed from a publication produced by the National Institute on Alcohol Abuse and Alcoholism), is a warning to those who act without appropriate knowledge and consultation regarding the facts. For those in religious leadership, the facts include such variables as the canonical rights of the impaired as well as the limits of authority. With respect to civil law, one should be familiar with the Americans with Disabilities Act when dealing with one who is also an employee. With respect to appropriate behavior, check the criteria and norms associated with the behavior or consumption of alcohol, drugs, food, spending, etc. Everyone should know the "policy" regarding addiction.

Ask yourself some of the following questions with respect to the use of alcohol and see if you can answer without some research. If you are an average person you may drink socially and consume moderate amounts of alcohol. If you are a woman over the age of 65, you have no more than one drink per day; if a man, you have no more than two drinks per day. More than these amounts could be putting you at risk. It may also be helpful to know at what level one is over the legal limit in his or her blood alcohol level. In general more than two drinks can impair driving and place someone at risk!

What is a drink?

A standard drink is:

- One 12-ounce bottle of beer or wine cooler

- One 5-ounce glass of wine

- 1.5 ounces of 80-proof distilled spirits.

Barriers to Effective Supervision

What are the things that get in the way when dealing with the problem person? What keeps me from effectively identifying, referring, and supervising the troubled person? These are questions every human being either at home, in the work place, or in their social life has asked him/herself. The reluctance to address the destructive or sometimes dangerous behaviors of others is sometimes referred to as "enabling."

Recognizing and Identifying Enabling

Enabling is any behavior, thoughts, feelings, and denial that protect another from the full consequences of their actions. The following is a self-examination regarding enabling.

Self-Examination for Enabling

1. Have I felt anger or hostility toward a problem person?
2. Have I spent too much time on trying to manage another?
3. Do I ever protect, or want to protect, a problem person?
4. Do I tend to feel pity and sympathy when someone complains of personal problems?
5. Do I become preoccupied or even obsessed with a problem person to the exclusion of attention to other matters?
6. Have I felt manipulated, used, and betrayed by the problem person's failure to improve?
7. Have I or am I aware of another taking over responsibilities for the impaired other?
8. Have I consciously avoided the problem person?
9. Have I lost sleep because of the situation?
10. Do I lack clear, definite standards of performance and professional conduct for those I am responsible to manage?
11. Have I gradually lowered my expectations for acceptable job performance with someone?
12. Do I avoid confrontation with others about poor performance or inappropriate behavior?
13. When I clearly observe addictive or compulsive behaviors at work or in community, do I avoid taking action?
14. When there is an unmistakable case of abuse or dependency, do I refuse to act for fear of not being supported by others?
15. Do I avoid confrontation for fear of losing my relationship with that person?
16. Do I think a certain amount of use or inappropriate behavior on the job is acceptable?
17. Do I believe that another's problem behavior or addiction is a private matter to be kept secret?
18. In looking for the reason for problems, do I tend to minimize addiction or compulsive behaviors?
19. Do I feel inadequate when someone promised to improve in their job performance and didn't?
20. I believe persons with addictions or compulsions can stop if they really want to?

Interpreting the Checklist

If you answered "sometimes" for any statement, you may have some attitudes that will get in the way of effective action.

If you answered "sometimes" to more than five statements, you may be seeing a clear pattern in yourself, the community or system, or both.

Enabling in the workplace is common. Very few even seasoned professionals can function without bias when dealing with their own members. The tendency is to minimize, deny, rationalize, not talk about it to others, complain, avoid, but the "DON'T TALK," "DON'T TRUST" and "DON'T FEEL" rules generally apply.

The remainder of this booklet is to inform and support those responsible for the supervision of the troubled religious and to the safety and trust of those served.

The Nature of Addictive Disorders

"When a trout rising to a fly gets hooked on a line and finds himself unable to swim freely...sometimes he masters his difficulties; sometimes they are too much for him. His struggles are all that the world sees and it naturally misunderstands them. It is hard for a free fish to understand what is happening to a hooked one." (Karl Menninger)

Name just about any behavior and I might be able to label it "addictive"! Some behaviors are considered "good addictions" and others are considered "bad habits." Some addictions are "self-destructive," and of course, some are "illegal" or lead to criminal prosecution and institutional liability. Ironically, with all the news about misconduct in the sexual arena, most problems especially in the United States criminal system are related to alcohol and other drugs and of

Paradox of The Alcoholic

By Austin Ripley
Founder of Guest House

The alcoholic (addict), of course, is many things, as we all know. He/She is the world's supreme paradox. Alcoholics drink, not because they would but because they must. They do not drink/addict for pleasure, they drink and addict to pain, yet they continue to addict. They will mortgage the wealth of the future to pay off the debts of the past so that they may drink up the non-existent present.

They are the only ones in nature, I think, who seek stimulation as a sedative, only to find that it acts upon the nerves as excited misery. They seek to inflate the puny little ego in the provocative wine of Bacchus and succeed in shriveling the soul in the bitter gall of remorse.

They escape desperately to free the self from the facts of reality and run headlong into the prison of fantasy. Success is just as fatal as failure to addicts. They will addict or drink with exhilaration to success and to sadness and misfortune. They addict or drink to get high in the evening, knowing how low they will be in the morning.

Bill Wilson, Founder of AA (right in photo), and Austin Ripley, Founder of Guest House, at Guest House, Lake Orion, Michigan

This booklet is sponsored by Guest House, Inc., a nonprofit, lay-governed organization dedicated exclusively to the care and treatment of Catholic clergy and religious suffering from addictive disorders and related problems. With treatment centers in Rochester, Minnesota, for men and Lake Orion, Michigan, for women, Guest House has served the Catholic Church in this sensitive and complicated area of health care since 1956. The Guest House mission includes the education and training of those in positions of ministry and leadership within the church regarding addiction, intervention, treatment, recovery, and prevention. To this end we encourage inquiries and requests for services as well as willing donors and benefactors interested in our work. All donations directly support the work of Guest House and are tax deductible under section 501 (c) (3) of the Internal Revenue Code.

these over 50 percent are alcohol related. Alcohol continues to be the great gateway drug and lowers inhibition allowing for the behaviors that one might otherwise never engage in.

The addictive process usually involves a series of *progressive* stages with incremental escalation in consumption and/or behavior until the individual loses control. The term *chronic* refers to the condition of no return, or the point when the person may never be able to drink normally again but has become dependent upon the substance or behavior. The behavioral addictions pose a very different problem in that some such as sexual compulsion or food addictions are involved with the person in a manner unlike substances or gambling that can be avoided by behavioral regulation and support.

With respect to alcohol, the term primary gives importance to the addiction in its own right and demands direct treatment knowing that unless the addictive process is arrested all other areas will continue to be impacted. Often there is greater physical damage than we realize and many will not stop until the illness has caused serious or permanent damage to the addict's health. This is particularly true of sexual addiction. Another major causative factor for intervention and treatment is legal and financial consequences. The nature of addiction is traumatic for all involved. There are no unaffected bystanders.

Diagnostic Criteria for Addictive Disorder

A maladaptive pattern of behavior and/or substance use, leading to significant impairment or distress, as manifested by three (or more) of the following, occurring at any time in the same 12-month period:

1. Tolerance, as defined by either of the following:
   A. A need for markedly increased amounts of the substance or behavior to achieve intoxication or desired effect.
   B. Markedly diminished effect with continued use or behavior at the same level.
2. Withdrawal, as manifested by either of the following:
   A. The characteristic withdrawal syndrome for the behavior or substance.

B. The same or another behavior or substance is used to avoid the withdrawal symptoms.
3. The substance or behavior is increased and/or over a longer period of time than was intended.
4. There is a persistent desire or unsuccessful efforts to cut down or control behavior or consumption of a substance.
5. A great deal of time is spent in activities necessary to engage in the behavior and/or obtain the substance.
6. Important social, occupational, or recreational activities are given up or reduced because of the addictive behavior and/or substance use.
7. The behavior or consumption is continued despite knowledge of having a persistent or recurrent physical or psychological problem that is likely to have been caused or exacerbated by the problem behavior and/or substance use.

The above criteria, adapted from *Diagnostic and Statistical Manuel of Mental Disorders, 4th Edition* (1994), are applicable to many behaviors and substances. Still, it is important to understand how frequent substance abuse and dependency are the primary disorder in so many other symptomatic behaviors and conditions.

A Word about Periodic Use and Abuse

Abuse is also defined as a "maladaptive pattern" characterized by hazardous or compulsive use or behavior, or the presence of role impairment or recurrent legal problems (these may be of a canonical or institutional nature!), but without evidence of tolerance or withdrawal. In short, abuse can be periodic or even occasional behavior that places the individual and/or others at risk. In many cases, those who abuse are likely to progress to chronic stages of dependency when allowed to continue unchecked. It is usually very difficult to convince one that something is a problem when it is engaged in only periodically or on certain dates. However, the majority of workplace accidents and risk occur with individuals who would meet criteria for abuse rather than dependency. A driver need only be intoxicated once to cause a major tragedy.

Signs and Symptoms of Addiction

1. In the Work Place

Absenteeism and lateness as well as unexplained absence are common. Often a pattern emerges as the individual loses control and the ability to regulate his or her behavior according to demands for responsible work behavior. The excuses and stories or explanations are often the next sign.

Dishonesty or lying is part of the denial process and resorts to rationalizations, denials, and minimizing often involving the blame of others and circumstance as excuse, rarely taking personal responsibility for shortcomings.

Some additional behavioral signs are: forgetting important dates and appointments, missing deadlines, poor decisions, lack of productivity, waste of resources, angry outbursts, threats to take action against the boss, refusal to take responsibility, requiring more supervision, failing to meet expectations that are demanded of peers, indiscretions regarding relationship with co-workers or others, secretive or elusive patterns regarding time management and use of resources.

These are particularly important with behavioral addictions such as gambling and sex addiction.

2. Psychological/Emotional Signs

Mood swings are the classic sign of an addictive process in the individual. Traditionally addictive substances and behaviors are learned and can be used to alter the individual's moods or emotional state. Addicts are poor regulators of emotions. In the addictive cycle, the greater the progression of the addiction the more likely the erratic nature of the mood swings. One might imagine watching your favorite team in the state championship in overtime only seconds away from defeat or victory. The addict is in this unstable emotional position frequently, if not regularly!

Some other signs are: depression, anxiety, paranoia, defiance, indifference, sarcasm, hyper-critical, avoidance, inability to focus, short term memory loss, impaired judgment and decision making skills, nervousness, distractibility, unfounded fears, inability to work with others, and isolation from others. Perhaps the hallmark psychological defense for the addict is denial and the use of projecting onto others personal responsibility. This defense system frequently is better identified as delusional as the addict has often convinced him or her it is the truth. You might say they "believe the lie."

3. Physical Signs

Physical signs can be addiction specific (i.e., alcohol on the breath or slurred speech), but others can be the result of many addictions: fatigue, frequent illnesses, overtired and sleepy, poor grooming, bruises or physical accidents, car accidents, walking into things and accidents in the work place due to the above, being distracted or disassociated, colds, infections, sexually transmitted disease, and depleted immune system often are consequence of the stress due to maintaining the addictive process as it takes a physical toll on the body.

4. Social or Relational Problems

Poor perceptions about how others see them, inappropriate comments and behaviors, lack of boundaries, sexual boundary violations, violence or abusive language, overreaction to others' comments or behaviors, poor communication (both in giving and receiving), undependable, judgmental, changes in companionship and friends, family problems, legal difficulties, financial issues such as borrowing money and failure to repay, embezzlement, negative and critical attitude toward others, refusing limits, avoiding supervisors and co-workers, complaints from others at work and community.

Identification and Intervention

Gather the facts in very clear terms that describe the specific concerns around behaviors and performance. These would include the inventory of possibilities listed above. Document what is being observed and include all relevant complaints from others. Consider the enabling checklist on page 71 and remember your limitations or liabilities in taking action.

It can also be very difficult to get the commitment of others to the identification process. No one wants to be the bad person or snitch! Do not try to handle the problem by yourself. Seek help and consultation from the beginning of the process.

If there is no immediate danger and the person is functioning but creating concern, (after consultation with a knowledgeable other) address the issues with the person and make things clear with respect to specific complaints. Make sure you document not only the meeting but also the expectations about what needs to improve. Consider a referral source for counseling help or evaluation and make a recommendation to a specific agency or professional with expertise in addiction intervention and treatment. Continue to monitor the individual for a significant time (perhaps six months to a year) to ensure he/she is following a course of remediation and improvement. Liability increases with knowledge and lack of supervision and containment!

Referral

Do: Refer individuals who are not functioning at appropriate levels as defined by norms for the group. Refer when you think counseling may be helpful. Refer when you simply can't get accurate information from the individual or believe you are not getting an honest self-appraisal. Remember that denial and dishonesty are part of the addictive process. Don't be misled by excuses, insist on answers that can be acceptable reasons, and when not forth-coming refer to the professional to evaluate for impairment.

- Use genuine concern and non-judgmental language without labeling or diagnosing the problem or person.
- Be prepared to be challenged or even attacked during the various stages of intervention.
- Maintain a support system to validate and affirm your role in the process.
- Remember, you are responsible "TO" the person not "FOR" the person's choices and consequences.
- Remember that identification and even treatment are only the initial stages of what may be a long-term process of recovery, rehabilitation, and possible misadventures and lapses along the way.

Do not: Consider discretion the better part of valor and wait until the problem is "out of control." It never gets easier, only more difficult as one bargains for the other to "get better." Do not get involved in the "personal business" of the person. Speak in non-specific terms and "feelings" or hearsay. Do not be harsh, accusatory, judgmental, threatening, or moralistic, such as asking "How could you?" type questions. Do not fail to follow up after the referral. Remember, in making the referral, to be clear about: The person's job performance and relationships with others. Has his/her performance and/or relationships deteriorated?

Intervention

What is intervention?

When the memory system has become thoroughly distorted for a long time and the defenses that have been erected seem impenetrable, outside intervention becomes necessary...Unless the destructive process is interrupted successfully, permanent disability and even premature death are inevitable. The intervention consists of a crises or series of crises that, in an objective, unequivocal, and nonjudgmental way, confront the alcoholic (addict), with the reality of the condition. (Johnson Institute, 1987)

The intervention process is best facilitated by an outside party who can be utilized as a resource for directly addressing the logistical matters as well as education, support, and the actual event if the need arises for a confrontation and referral for treatment or help. The basic ingredients for a successful intervention involve the following:

- Be prepared with the facts regarding areas of impairment or problems as identified and documented.
- Know your institutional policies regarding performance as well as substance use and misconduct.
- Consult with a canon lawyer even when you are confident you are on solid ground. Addicts can become extremely threatening when challenged!

- Know the nature of the problem, whether it is a behavioral addiction and substances, alcohol or food and some basic clinical aspects of the illness and associated features, i.e., concurrent medical, psychological conditions.
- Gather appropriate and informed others if needed to be part of the process.
- Be very clear about what is being presented and the directives for the impaired person regarding treatment, evaluation, and continuing care.
- Be prepared to deal with refusal to comply by the addict and know what alternatives are acceptable, if any.
- Have a series of resources for evaluation and treatment to offer some choice to the person, if needed.
- Know the various levels and types of care for the specific problems.
- Be sensitive to the added burden for the clergy and religious in admitting the need for help. This is true of most helping professionals and ministers.
- Be aware of the risks for the person regarding vocation and career.
- Realize how the addictive process has become a major part of the person's coping mechanism and, while destructive, may be the last thing the addict has to depend upon.

Religious Culture and Direct Address

In studies of alcoholism among the clergy it is a common complaint that the disease is allowed to continue far beyond the time when it is first recognized as a problem. In one study of several hundred Guest House men, drinking continued for an average of eight years after identification by others. The alcoholic was aware for an even longer period of time (Donovan, 1989). If we consider other possible addictions and areas of impairment, all of us can think of cases involving others who where or are allowed to continue in a destructive behavior without direct confrontation or consequences. Common themes among the religious and clergy are those of vocation, spirituality, ecclesial, and spirituality (Fichter, 1982).

> **"It may seem more difficult at times to deal with the ongoing issues as they emerge than it was in the original intervention. This means that treatment, aftercare, continuing care, and affiliation with a recovery network and supports are critical for the addict as well as the community and superior or diocese."**

The stigma attached to the impaired religious is considered greater due to the vocational aspects. The ecclesial domain involves authority and the hierarchical paradigm of authority at the top, however, there is frequently a lack of knowledge by the person in authority of the particulars, or lack of experience in dealing with the issues of addiction. The vocational nature of priesthood or religious life makes the claim of a higher estate in the sense one is theoretically more responsible to be, and do well. Finally, spirituality is at the heart of the religious vocation and addiction is defined in part as a spiritual illness.

In understanding the illness or the addiction and its particular signs and symptoms, it is equally important to understand the person laboring under the influence of the illness and what factors may inhibit both the intervention process and surrender to treatment by the impaired other. The above-mentioned aspects of religious culture lend themselves to the rules of don't talk, trust, or feel. This creates a barrier between the troubled person and others as well as between those who may be concerned about the behavior. These rules may be even more damaging in the continuing care phase of recovery and the need for monitoring and supervision. The intervention process is a challenge to all of these norms!

The good news is that church institutions are far more responsive in recent history to identification and intervention, but there is much that needs to be done to maintain a healthy and open system for the inevitable incidence of addiction among religious and clergy, (probably equal to the general population between 10 and 12%).

The other good news is that recovering religious and clergy are often better and more effective as a result of their experience and can be valuable resources for prevention, intervention, and support for other clergy and religious as well as those served.

Treatment, Recovery, Monitoring and Supervision

The issues that apply to identification and intervention in the beginning continue to be part of the recovery and reintegration process for both the impaired and the responsible authority. It may seem more difficult at times to deal with the ongoing issues as they emerge than it was in the original intervention. This means that treatment, aftercare, continuing care, and affiliation with a recovery network and supports are critical for the addict as well as the community and superior or diocese.

The process starts with treatment, usually a period of time apart from the context of the problem and a complete physical, psychological, and social evaluation. Denial around the behaviors is addressed and alternative ways of coping and dealing with problems are explored and learned. Affiliation with recovery resources such as twelve-step groups and continuing-care groups are experienced. Often an alumni network of the rehabilitation center is introduced for the return home. The level of treatment, i.e., inpatient, hospital cares, etc., is usually determined by the severity of the condition and involves an initial period of evaluation. It is particularly important to assess for medical conditions followed by potential threats for self-destructive behavior or harm to others, and physical withdrawal when there is potential for life threatening complications such as alcohol withdrawal in certain individuals. Physical complications as a result of the problem are usually very good reason for residential care and medical monitoring. Infections, nutritional deficiencies, and a variety of system and organ pathologies are common with addiction. The length of treatment is relative to certain criteria that the treatment agency should be able to justify as necessary based upon the individual's condition and the recovery environment as a safe place of return. A time of healing and restoration particularly in terms of physical well being can be critical to long term recovery. It is also hoped that the person will have spiritual experience that sets them on a new path.

It is recommended that those involved in the life and work of the addicted person may also need help and support. The addictive process affects everyone and there are several ANON groups for support for the non-addict. Knowing how to live in recovery can be as challenging to others as to the impaired person. Usually the treatment facility involves responsible authority in the aftercare and discharge process.

Supervision and monitoring involve diplomacy, respecting confidentiality, and responsibility to the individual and for the good of the order, diocese, and others. It is important to talk to the person not about the person. Assessment of progress is usually the responsibility of ongoing treatment providers, an identified personnel person, and the responsible concern of those involved in the individual's life and work. The idea is to be understanding but to hold the person accountable to the agreed upon plan and reporting requirements as documented. When problems arise address them directly in a non-judgmental manner and involve the treatment professional or personnel person if necessary.

Almost a half-century ago, Austin Ripley founded Guest House with what at that time was a revolutionary mission—to treat religious and clergy who suffer from alcoholism. Ripley believed it was essential to treat men in an atmosphere affirming the nature of priesthood and religious life. He also knew that the most effective approach for addiction is the Twelve Steps in treating a disease that is physical, spiritual, and emotional or psychological.

Since then, Guest House has treated more than 6,300 priests, deacons, brothers, and seminarians to be released from the malady of addiction. Guest House provides a special community atmosphere for men and women suffering from addiction. These men and women have learned that they are not alone and that the identification of addiction can be turned from a source of shame and self-destruction into the first step toward a happy and productive and purposeful life. Guest House has been a resource for the suffering addict as well as the church and those who minister within its ranks.

Information and consultation Services
Education & Training
Policy development
Free Help for Alcohol and
Related Problems

Priests
Deacons
Religious Women & Men
Seminarians
Church personnel

To Obtain Information or Services,
Call 1-800-626-6910/1-800-634-4155
Guest House, Inc.
P.O. 420
Lake Orion, MI 48361

www.guesthouse.org

APPENDIX

List of Readings for Intervention, Treatment and Recovery

Addictions and Ministry Formation

There are many helps in printed format, on the Web, in church publications, and in numerous institutions and agencies that regularly publish articles and books for those responsible for the monitoring and supervision of others. The business of caring for another is not always as efficient and simple as we would like. The effort to be responsible to the person and at the same time one's self and others is at best demanding. The greatest asset to help you in this endeavor will be your policy and procedures manual as a rational guide to what is often an emotional roller coaster. Well developed and implemented policies and procedures with adequate support and consultation takes the worry out of much guessing and personal anxiety about your obligations and limitations. The following are a few suggestions for further reading and study provided by Guest House.

Bishop's Committee on Priestly Life and Ministry. *Recommendations and an Enquiry about Alcoholism among Catholic Clergy.* Washington, DC: United States Catholic Conference, 1978.

Bryant, Kathleen, RSC. *Vocations Anonymous: A Handbook for Adults Discerning Priesthood and Religious Life.* Chicago, IL: National Coalition for Church Vocations, 1996.

Canon Law Society of America. *Procedural Handbook for Institutes of Consecrated Life and Societies of Apostolic Life.* Washington, DC, 2001.

Canon Law Society of America, edited by Calvo & Klinger. *Clergy Procedural Handbook.* Washington, DC, 1992.

Carnes, Patrick, Ph.D., guest editor. *Special Issue: Medical Aspects of Sexual Addiction/Compulsivity,* American Journal of Preventive Psychiatry & Neurology, Vol. 2, No. 3 (May 1990).

Blair, Linda. *The Supervisor's Role in Early Recovery.* Minneapolis, MN: Johnson Institute, 1991.

Fichter, Joseph, SJ. *The Rehabilitation of Alcoholic Clergy; Ardent Spirits Subdued.* New York: Human Science Press, 1982.

Friberg, N., and M. Lasser, *Before the Fall, Preventing Pastoral Sexual Abuse.* Collegeville, MN: The Liturgical Press, 1998.

Furton, J. Edward, and Veronica McCloud Dort, eds. *Addiction and Compulsive Behaviors: Proceedings of the Seventeenth Workshop for Bishops.* Boston, MA: The National Catholic Bioethics Center, 2000.

Grant, Robert, Ph.D. *Healing the Soul of the Church: Ministers Facing Their Own Childhood Abuse and Trauma.* Oakland, CA, 1994. Contact information: rw_grant@hotmail.com.

Johnson, Vernon. *I'll Quit Tomorrow.* Harper San Francisco, 1980.

King, Eleace, IHM, Ed.D. and Castelli, J. *Culture of Recovery, Culture of Denial, Alcoholism Among Men and Women Religious.* Washington, DC: Center for Applied Research in the Apostolate, 1995.

May, Gerald, M.D. *Addiction and Grace.* New York: Harper & Row, 1988.

National Catholic Clergy Council on Alcoholism. *Alcoholism: A Source Book for the Priest, An Anthology.* Indianapolis, IN, 1960.

NOCERCC. *Priestly Relationships: Freedom Through Boundaries.* Chicago, IL: National Organization for the Continuing Education of Roman Catholic Clergy, Inc., 1997.

Papesh, Michael. *Clerical Culture Contradiction and Transformation.* Collegeville, MN: Liturgical Press, 2004.

Rutter, Peter, MD. *Sex in the Forbidden Zone.* Los Angeles, CA: Tarcher, Inc., 1989.

SAMHSA, Substance Abuse and Mental Health Services, Office of Applied Studies, U.S. Department of Health and Human Services, Rockville, MD. http://www.oas.samhsa.gov.

Sammon, Sean, FMS. *Alcoholism's Children, ACoAs in Priesthood and Religious Life.* Staten Island, New York, 1989.

Schoener, G., et al. *Sexual Exploitation by Clergy in Psychotherapists' Sexual Involvement with Clients: Intervention and Prevention.* Minneapolis, MN: Walk-In Counseling Center, 1989.

Stratman, Bernard, SM, ed. "Seminary Journal Special Section on Addiction," *Seminary Journal,* Vol. 9, No. 3 (2003), Washington, DC: National Catholic Education Association.

Fellowships Similar to Alcoholic Anonymous

The "anonymous" organizations are listed below for information purposes only. In keeping with its Sixth tradition, Alcoholics Anonymous does not "endorse, finance, or lend the A.A. name to any related facility or outside enterprise, lest problems of money, property, and prestige divert us from our primary purpose."

Adult Children of Alcoholics (ACA)
P.O. Box 3216
Torrance, CA 90510
(310) 534-1815 (messages)
Email: info@adultchildren.org
Web: www.adultchildren.org

Al-Anon/Alateen Family Group Headquarters
(for families and friends of alcoholics)
1600 Corporate Landing Pkwy.
Virginia Beach, VA 23454-5617
(757) 563-1600
(888) 425-2666 (general meeting info)

FAX: (757) 563-1655
Email: wso@al-anon.org
Web: www.al-anon.alateen.org

A.R.T.S. Anonymous
(Artists Recovering through the Twelve Steps)
P.O. Box 230175
New York, NY 10023
(212) 873-7075
Web: www.artsanonymous.org

Clutters Anonymous
P.O. Box 91413
Los Angeles, CA 90009-1413

Cocaine Anonymous
3740 Overland Ave, Suite C
Los Angeles, CA 90034-6337
(310) 559-5833
FAX: (310) 559-2554
Email: cawso@ca.org
Web: www.ca.org

CoDA (Co-Dependents Anonymous)
P.O. Box 33577
Phoenix, AZ 85067-3577
(602) 277-7991
Web: www.codependents.org

Debtors Anonymous
P.O. Box 920888
Needham, MA 02492-0009
(781) 453-2743
FAX: (781) 453-2745
Email: new@debtorsanonymous.org

Emotions Anonymous
P.O. Box 4245
St. Paul, MN 55104-0245
(651) 647-9712
FAX: (651) 647-1593
Email: info@emotionsanonymous.org

Gamblers Anonymous
P.O. Box 17173
Los Angeles, CA 90017
(213) 386-8789
FAX: (213) 386-0030
Email: isomain@gamblersanonymous.org
Web: www.gamblersanonymous.org

I.S.A. (Incest Survivors Anonymous)
P.O. Box 17245
Long Beach, CA 90807-7245
(562) 428-5599
Email: bb239@lafn.org

N.A. (Narcotics Anonymous)
P.O. Box 9999
Van Nuys, CA 91409-9999
(818) 773-9999
FAX (818) 700-0700
Email: info@na.org
Web: www.na.org/contact.htm

Nicotine Anonymous
419 Main Street PMB #370
Huntington Beach, CA 92648
(866)536-4539
FAX (714) 969-4493
Email: info@nicotine-anonymous.org

Obsessive Compulsive Anonymous
P.O. Box 215
New Hyde Park, NY 11040
(516) 739-0662 (recorded message)
Web: http://hometown.aol.com/west24th/index.html?f=fs

O.A. (Overeaters Anonymous)
P.O. Box 44020
Rio Rancho,NM 87174-4020
(505) 891-2664
FAX (505) 891-4320
Web: www.oa.org/index.htm

P.A.A. (Pill Addicts Anonymous)
P.O. Box 13728
Reading, PA 19612

Positive Anonymous (HIV Positive)
453 North Pearl Street
Albany, NY 12204
(518) 436-3465

S.A.A. (Sex Addicts Anonymous)
P.O. Box 70949
Houston, TX 77270
(800) 477-8191 (calls from U.S./Canada)
(713) 869-4902 (from outside U.S./Canada)
Email: info@saa-recover.org
Web: www.saa-recovery.org

Sex and Love Addicts Anonymous
(The Augustine Fellowship)
P.O. Box 338
Norwood, MA 02062-0338
(781) 255-8825 (leave a message)
Email: slaaoffice@slaafws.org

Sexaholics Anonymous
P.O. Box 111910
Nashville, TN 37222-1910
(615) 331-6230
FAX (615) 331-6901
Email: saico@sa.org
Web: www.sa.org

S.I.A. (Survivors of Incest Anonymous)
World Service Office
P.O. Box 190
Benson, MD 21018
(410) 893-3322
Web: www.siawso.org

Workaholics Anonymous
P.O. Box 289
Menlo Park, CA 94026-0289
(510) 273-9253 (leave a message)
Email: wawso@yahoo.com

New Jersey Self-Help Clearinghouse
(for NJ and national information)
100 E. Hanover Ave., 2nd Floor
Cedar Knolls, NJ 07297
(973) 326-6789 (for callers outside of NJ)
(800) 367-6274 (for callers from within NJ)
FAX (973) 326-9467
Web: www.njgroups.org

National Self-Help Clearinghouse
(information for all areas)
Graduate School & University Center of the
City
University of New York
365 Fifth Avenue, Suite 3300
New York, NY 10016
(212) 817-1822
Web: www.selfhelpweb.org

New York City Self-Help Center
(information for NYC only)
120 West 57th Street
New York, NY 10019
(212) 586-5770

Self-Help Information Network Exchange
Scranton Life Building
538 Spruce Street, Suite 420
Scranton, PA 18503
(570) 961-1234 (9:00 am-4:30 pm, Mon.-Fri.)

Neruoticos Anonimos (Neurotics Anonymous)
A.C., Oficina de Servicios Generales
Apartado Postal M-9355
Mexico City, D.F. 06000, Mexico
(52) 55-12-43-83 & (52) 55-12-37-74
FAX (52) 55-12-63-44
Email: naac@prodigy.net.mx
Material available in Spanish and English

CORE ELEMENT *SERIES* ORDER FORM

SPONSOR OPTION

Become a project sponsor at one of the following levels. You will receive copies of Volumes 1-4 and provide financial support for the ongoing development of this *Core Elements* series.

- ❏ Level #1 = $100 (2 copies of each of Volumes 1-4 in the series)
- ❏ Level #2 = $250 (4 copies of Volumes 1-4)
- ❏ Level #3 = $500 (5 copies of Volumes 1-4, plus a 50% discount on the <u>first</u> series purchase)

PURCHASE COPIES

The price per set of volumes 1-4 is $27.00; volumes in *Core Elements* series are $8.00 each.

Quantity discounts apply when ordering more than 5 sets or 12 individual copies.
(Shipping & Handling will be added to international orders; prepaid orders over $80.00; and orders requiring an invoice.)

PRICE PER SET: 1-5 sets = $27.00 each
                      6-9 sets = $24.00 each
                      10 plus sets = $23.00 each

PRICE PER COPY: 1-12 copies = $8.00 each
                      13-32 copies = $6.00 each
                      33 plus copies = $5.00 each

____ SETS OF 4 VOLUMES (CE1-CE4) in the *Core Elements* series

____ CE1 Theological Foundation and Cultural Understandings for Seminary Formation
____ CE2 Human and Spiritual Formation
____ CE3 Intellectual and Pastoral Formation
____ CE4 Addictions and Ministry Formation
____ *SEMINARY JOURNAL*: $20.00 USA; $32.00 International (3 issues per year: Spring, Fall, Winter)

ORDER TOTAL $

❏ Check enclosed (Made Payable to NCEA)
❏ Credit Card (MasterCard/Visa ONLY) ❏ MasterCard   ❏ Visa

Name on Card: _____   Phone: _____

Card Number: _____   Expiration Date   E-Mail: _____

❏ Send Invoice (*S&H will be added to invoice.*)

Name _____   Institution _____

Address _____   P.O. Box _____   Country _____

City _____   State/Province _____   Postal Code _____

Mail To:
NCEA Seminary Department • 1077 30ᵗʰ Street, NW, Suite 100 • Washington, DC 20007-3852
Fax: (202) 333-6706 • Phone: (202) 337-6232, Ext. 222 • E-Mail: seminary@ncea.org

SEMINARY JOURNAL ORDER FORM

T he *Seminary Journal* is a journal of opinion, research, and praxis in the field of seminary education and formation for priesthood within the Roman Catholic tradition.

Articles are selected, edited, and published by the Executive Director of the Seminary Department of the National Catholic Educational Association.

The *Seminary Journal* is published three times each year, in the spring, fall, and winter. NCEA Seminary Department dues entitle member institutions to four copies of the *Seminary Journal*, addressed to the president/rector, the academic dean, the director of formation, and the librarian.

Individual subscriptions may be ordered at $20.00 per year. Single copies of current or back issues may be purchased for $7.50 each.

Bulk rate is available for members. Ten or more copies: $3.50 each.

MAIL completed ORDER form TO:
NCEA Seminary Department
1077 30th Street, NW, Suite 100
Washington, DC 20007-3852
(202) 337-6232, ext. 222 • fax (202) 333-6706
seminary@ncea.org

ORDER FORM for the Seminary Journal

Name_____

Address_____

City_____

State_____ Zip_____

Telephone _____

E-mail _____

Subscriptions - $20.00 per year.
Shipping & Handling for U.S. deliveries is Library Rate and included in the price of the publication. S&H for international subscriptions is $12.00 for International Economy Mail service or $20.00 for Airmail Print Matter service.

❏ Please begin my subscription to the *Seminary Journal*.
❏ I would like to renew my subscription.
❏ Shipping for International Subscribers only: (Check)
    ❏ Airmail Printed Matter = add $20.00
    ❏ Economy Mail = add $12.00

BULK Orders, BACK Issues, STANDING Orders
1-5 copies - $7.50 each
6-9 copies - $5.00 each
10 or more copies - $3.50 each

❏ I would like to place a BULK order for
_____ copies of Vol._____ No._____

❏ I would like to place an order for the following BACK issues:

_____ copies of Vol. _____ No. _____
_____ copies of Vol. _____ No. _____
_____ copies of Vol. _____ No. _____
_____ copies of Vol. _____ No. _____

❏ I would like to place a STANDING order for _____ copies of the *Journal* for the volume year (Spring, Fall, Winter). A renewal notice will be included with the Winter shipment. See pricing schedule: cost of publications plus S&H will be invoiced.

For an Index of Volumes since 1995, e-mail: seminary@ncea.org *or visit:* www.ncea.org/departments/seminary/resources.asp.

Shipping & Handling for Quantity Orders
For U.S. (domestic) shipments: For 1-9 copies add $6.00 per order. Orders for 10 or more copies will be invoiced for S&H costs.

For international subscribers only, check one:
    ❏ Airmail Printed Matter
    ❏ Economy Mail (allow 4-6 weeks for delivery)

Order Summary

Subtotal: _____ S&H (if known):_____

TOTAL AMOUNT DUE: _____

❏ Payment Enclosed (Make check or money order payable to NCEA)
❏ Send Invoice ❏ Credit Card (see below)

All orders less than $20.00 must be prepaid. If applicable, S&H charges will be added to above total before processing or an invoice sent.

Credit Card   ❏ MasterCard   ❏ Visa

Card Number_____

Exp. Date _____

Name on Card_____

Signature _____